Thomas Wolfe's Purdue Speech
"Writing and Living"

14

About this time, I began to write. I was editor
of the college paper- which, in my day, and under my
direction, always did have, at least, a certain archaeological
interest) since it was interesting to examine in this
week's edition the ruins and relics of last month's news.
But in addition to this, I wrote some stories and some
poems for the magazine, of which I was also a member of
the editorial staff. The War was going on then; I was too
young to be in service, and ⊥ suppose my first attempts
creatively may be traced to the direct and patriotic
inspiration of the War. I remember one, in particular-
a poem, (I believe, my first) which was aimed dimentipxai
directly at the luckless head of Kaiser Bill. The poem
was called defiantly "The Challenge", and ⊥ remember
it was written directly in the style, and according to
the meter, of the Present Crisis," by James Russell Lowell.
I remember further that it took a high tone from the very
beginning: the poet, it is said, is the phrophetwtund-
prophet and the bard- the awakened tongue of all his folk-
and ⊥ was all of that. In the name of embattled democracy,
I let the Kaiser have the works, and I remember two lines
in particular that seemed to me to have a very ringing tone-
"Thoux hast given us the challenge- pay, now dog, the cost,
and go!" I remember these lines so well because they were
the occasion of an editorial argument at the time: the
more mxmxmxmxmx conservative element on the editorial
staff, felt that the words, "thou dog" were too mxmxm

Frontispiece: A page of Wolfe's original typescript of the Purdue Speech, showing his own handwritten corrections

Thomas Wolfe's Purdue Speech
"Writing and Living"

edited from the dictated and revised
typescript with an introduction and notes by

WILLIAM BRASWELL
and
LESLIE A. FIELD

1964
Purdue University Studies

©1964 by Purdue Research Foundation
Library of Congress Catalog No. 64-63462

ACKNOWLEDGMENTS

It is a pleasure to acknowledge the assistance of those who have contributed toward the preparation of this monograph. To Mr. Paul Gitlin, Administrator CTA of the Estate of Thomas Wolfe, we are indebted for permission to publish the Purdue speech. We are grateful to Mr. William H. Bond, curator of manuscripts of the Houghton Library of Harvard University, for access to the Thomas Wolfe Collection of William B. Wisdom and especially for his finding four missing pages of the dictated typescript of the speech. Mr. William S. Powell, librarian of the North Carolina Collection of the University of North Carolina, was helpful and kind both in person and by correspondence. Miss Myra Champion, of the Pack Memorial Public Library of Asheville, answered questions and offered fruitful suggestions.

Mrs. Peter Campbell, formerly Miss Gwenn Jassinoff, very graciously provided information about her experience as Wolfe's last secretary. Among authorities on Wolfe we are obligated for answers to questions and for helpful suggestions to C. Hugh Holman, who read the manuscript, and to Richard S. Kennedy and Floyd C. Watkins. For details about Wolfe's speeches in Colorado we are indebted to professors W. F. Dyde and John Wrenn and Miss Bernadine Smith, of the University of Colorado, and Professor John Harrison, of Colorado State College at Greeley. Professor Dougald MacMillan and Registrar Raymond W. Leonard, of the University of North Carolina, and Mrs. B. C. Jones, Mr. Ellis C. Jones, and Mrs. Raymond W. Leonard, all of North Carolina, very kindly answered questions about Wolfe's friend B. C. Jones. Among colleagues at Purdue who gave aid and encouragement were Hugo Reichard, Richard Voorhees, Harold Watts, Raney Stanford, and William Stafford. We appreciate the care and patience of our editor, Mrs. Robin Friedheim. To the School of the Humanities, Social Science, and Education and to the Department of English at Purdue we are indebted for duplicating and typing services.

We are happy to express our appreciation to *College English* for permission to reprint "Thomas Wolfe Lectures and Takes a Holiday," to Charles Scribner's Sons for permission to quote from *The Letters of Thomas Wolfe* (ed. Elizabeth Nowell) and Hayden Norwood's *The Marble Man's Wife,* and to Doubleday and Company, Inc., for permission to quote from Elizabeth Nowell's *Thomas Wolfe: A Biography.*

W. B.
L. A. F.

CONTENTS

INTRODUCTION

In the early and middle nineteen-thirties Carl Sandburg, Sherwood Anderson, and Theodore Dreiser were among the speakers at Purdue University's annual Literary Awards Banquet, at which prizes were awarded to winners in the student literary contest. On March 30, 1938, the chairman of the committee responsible for the program sent a telegram to Thomas Wolfe asking him to speak at the dinner on May 19. The invitation caught him at the right time and in the right mood.

Wolfe had refused to become a regular lecturer. "I am a writer and not a public speaker," he protested in one of his many refusals to speak publicly, "and if I have anything at all to say to people I will have to say it through writing or not at all." He had turned down offers "to give lectures and to go on lecture tours which would have paid . . . thousands of dollars. . . . I have never in my life gone around making speeches at public gatherings and I do not intend to begin it now."[1]

But he did give occasional talks. On visits to North Carolina in 1937 he spoke informally to the class of an old friend in Chapel Hill and to civic clubs in Asheville. And in the summer of 1935, on the way to his first tour of the West, he was a featured speaker at the Writers' Conference at the University of Colorado.

The invitation from Purdue came when he needed a vacation. For the last seven months he had been hard at work again on what he referred to as "the book," and for some time he had been looking forward to a break. Now he had firmly in mind the structure of the long narrative about George Webber, and in the intervening weeks before

---

[1] Letter to V. F. Calverton, April 3, 1936, in *The Letters of Thomas Wolfe*, ed. Elizabeth Nowell (New York: Charles Scribner's Sons, 1956), pp. 497-498.

the lecture he could organize the vast amount of manuscript material well enough to leave it with an untroubled
conscience while he took a holiday in the West. There was
of course still much work to be done on the manuscript,
as Edward Aswell discovered when, after Wolfe's death,
he quarried out of it *The Web and the Rock* and *You
Can't Go Home Again* as well as the pieces in *The Hills
Beyond*.

Wolfe's success as a speaker in Colorado gave him confidence for the affair at Purdue. In Greeley, where he gave
a warm-up talk at the Colorado State College of Education,
and in Boulder, where he addressed the Writers' Conference for an hour and forty minutes, he had been highly
praised by the local press. In both places he spoke without
notes, but he drew heavily on the substance of what appeared shortly afterward as *The Story of a Novel*. At the
Writers' Conference, the University of Colorado *Silver and
Gold* reported, "He did not try to hold himself to a set
speech but seemed to burst upon the stage and allow
all he wanted to say to be said." The article leaves no
doubt about the impact of the talk on the audience: "Amid
the thunderous and truly sincere applause that burst forth
when the young genius sat down, Edward Davison [Direc-
tor of the Conference] rose to say that here at last was a
genuine expression of the New American Art."[2] Wolfe
recalled the event with pleasure in a letter about the coming engagement at Purdue.

To collect his thoughts for the talk at Purdue, he dictated a speech to his secretary. Mrs. Peter Campbell, then
Miss Gwen Jassinoff, says that when she went to work as
Wolfe's secretary, he wrote everything out in longhand
and then had her type it; but after she had been with him
a few weeks, she told him that she could take dictation
directly at the typewriter, and they followed that procedure
from then on. According to Edward Aswell, Wolfe never
hesitated for a word when writing longhand; Mrs. Campbell says that he was equally fluent when dictating: "The
words poured from him, and until I learned that he had

---

[2] University of Colorado *Silver and Gold,* August 8, 1935.

worked them over in his mind for hours, even days, before he started to dictate, I was flabbergasted. I couldn't understand how he did it, and I asked him about it. He said: 'I write them in my mind first.' "

At that time Wolfe was living in New York in the Hotel Chelsea, on 23rd Street, where he had a bedroom, a bathroom, a living room, and a small room in which his secretary worked. Mrs. Campbell gives a picture of him dictating: "My typewriter was on a typing table next to a window fronting on the street, and next to it was a tall chest. When he dictated, Wolfe would either stand beside me, leaning on the chest, or he would pace furiously back and forth between the living room and the small room. The thing I especially enjoyed was when he would act out the part he was dictating, much as an actor reading his lines."[3]

Since Wolfe usually dictated ten or fifteen pages a day, Mrs. Campbell estimates that it took him about five days to do the 63-page speech. Apparently he had finished it by May 3 because a letter written on that day refers to it as an accomplished fact.

He also mentioned it two days later in a letter to Professor F. A. Cummings, chairman of the program at Purdue: "I have already written down in very simple form what I want to say—just for the sake of getting it objectively stated. But I do not think I will even refer to a typed page, when I get up to talk, because I think I may do better without it." He tells what he has in mind. He wants to make this "a kind of 'workshop talk'—that is, a very simple account of a writer's work and his beliefs and convictions about writing, drawn directly from his own experience." He goes on to say that in *The Story of a Novel,* written almost three years earlier, he had summarized his writing experience up to that time. "I think there has been another development since then, and with your permission I should like to try to tell about it in my talk. It is this:

---

[3] Letters from Mrs. Peter Campbell to the editors, May 16 and July 7, 1962.

"In the past three years, in particular, I have thought more and more of the writer's relation to the world around him, and what effect it has, or ought to have, on his work. Briefly, my own experience, which I think is fairly typical of many writers, has been this: I began life, as many young men do, as a lyrical writer. That is, I wanted to express my vision of life and of the world largely in terms of my own youth and my own personality. At college and later on, when I first began to write, I went through one of the usual periods of aesthetics—that is, seeing the life of the artist and his work in aesthetic terms: perhaps you could call it a somewhat 'ivory tower' view of things. As I grew older, and as I continued to work, my view began to change, and I think this, too, was natural and inevitable. That is to say, as I grew older, I think I was not so much preoccupied with the concerns and purposes of my own youth. The field of my objectivity widened—with greater maturity and experience, I believe I began to look at the life around me more objectively—to see things and people and the world in a more objective way."

He wants to show the students that "the writer is not a strange and mysterious creature, but very definitely a citizen of mankind, a living, breathing, acting member of the human race, with work to do, a place to fill, a function to perform like everyone." He suggests as a title for his talk "Writing and Living," the title under which it was announced.[4]

In his letter of May 3 to Miss Elizabeth Nowell, his literary agent for periodical publications, Wolfe went into considerably more detail about the typescript he had dictated, showing that he regarded it not merely as notes for incidental remarks to aspiring young writers but as a very important statement about himself. He tells her that he finally rejected the proposal of the editors of *The Nation* that he contribute a 3,000-word essay on his philosophy of life to a series that was to be published first in the periodical and then in a book entitled *Living Philosophies*.

---

[4] *Letters*, pp. 755-757.

"At the same time I made another suggestion to them. I told them about the Purdue engagement, and told them that I proposed to go out and talk to the students right out of the workshop, so to speak—to tell them what I thought and felt about writing, what I think I have learned about it, what change and development has come about in me, and what convictions and beliefs I now have, not only about writing, but about the life around me from which I draw the sources of my materials, and the writer's place in the whole world today."

This subject, he says, has been his principal interest for at least a year now, beginning with the piece on Nazi tyranny that he published in *The New Republic*, "I Have a Thing to Tell You," and coming up to his present work. "I believe the time has come when I am ready to say it, and if the time has come and I can say it, it will knock the *New Republic* piece into a cocked hat because it will shoot the works.

"What I did, therefore, first of all, was simply to dictate a very plain and simple account of things to use at the Purdue gathering. Of course, it is immensely too long, and besides toward the end there are many, many things in it of too personal and complex a nature for an occasion of that sort." *The Nation* suggested that he show them the Purdue piece in its present form, but he declined temporarily; if he did do anything for them, he estimated that it would come closer to being 30,000 words than 3,000, which would probably make it unsuitable for the periodical.

He goes on to reveal that before he completed his dictation he was thinking not so much about the address at Purdue or an article for *The Nation* as about the conclusion of his forthcoming novel. "For months now, it has occurred to me that I would conclude the tremendously long book on which I am working with a kind of epilogue that takes the form of personal address. . . . That epilogue, as I have conceived it, would be a kind of impassioned summing up of the whole book, of everything that has gone before, and a final statement of what is now. The book will certainly close in some such way as this, although it may turn out at the end that the method of personal address, even in high poetic terms, is not the best way to conclude a book in which the whole narrative, hundreds of characters, and the events of more than a hundred years are stated objectively. However that may be, it is not important here, for if I succeed in doing [the epilogue] . . . as I want to do it, it will stand most tremendously on its own legs. Anyway, that is what I am doing now: transforming the material for the simple Purdue statement into the terms of poetic and imaginative fact—into the truth of fiction—because it seems to me that is really my essential job.''[5]

His awareness toward the end of the dictated statement that he was going to use some of it in the novel is shown in his addressing his remarks not to "students . . . here in Indiana," as in the beginning, but to "dear friend"—the dear friend being Foxhall Edwards (Maxwell Perkins), to whom George Webber (Thomas Wolfe) writes the long letter that constitutes the epilogue of *You Can't Go Home Again*. Here he has clearly given up dictating the speech and is definitely working on the conclusion of his novel. And despite what he said in the letter to Miss Nowell, there is even the possibility that here in his dictation he is drawing on material already formulated for the narrative. Many pages of the typescript, marked and revised in Wolfe's hand, show him in the process of adapting passages for the novel. Some of the revisions were elementary, such as changes in names: "Chapel Hill" to "Pine Rock" and "Scott Fitzgerald" to "Hunt Conroy." Many others afford subtler evidence of the artist at work, reorganizing, telescoping, eliminating words, sentences, and whole sections. As Aswell remarked, Wolfe had become "a tireless reviser and rewriter."[6] (On revisions of the typescript see Appendix I.)

Working feverishly those last few days before setting out for the Midwest, Wolfe together with his secretary got the tremendous manuscript of his novel into order that pleased

---

[5] *Letters,* pp. 750-752.

[6] Edward Aswell, "A Note on Thomas Wolfe," in Thomas Wolfe, *The Hills Beyond* (New York: Harper and Brothers, 1941), p. 355.

him for the time being. He planned much more work on it, but he was happy to get away from it for a while.

When Wolfe spoke at Purdue, he did not use a manuscript. So far as is known, no one took notes on what he said. The accounts of the affair in the Purdue *Exponent* and the Lafayette *Journal and Courier* indicated that the audience was very appreciative, but reported little of the speech. A few months later, after Wolfe's death, William Braswell, a Purdue staff member who had heard the speech, wrote an article giving his impressions of Wolfe as a speaker and recording some of the things that he and his friends remembered Wolfe's saying, both in his address and in conversation during the following week end. (The article is reprinted in Appendix II.) As Wolfe had remarked, the typescript contained much more than he had time to say in the fifty minutes or so that he spoke at the dinner, but the article about the occasion indicates that he did speak out of his own experience and that he used at least much of the first part of the dictated material. It also leaves no doubt about the impression he gave of earnestness and sincerity. He himself was well pleased over the outcome: "Everything went off beautifully at Purdue—I talked and talked, there was great applause, and everyone seemed satisfied."[7]

When the late Elizabeth Nowell was collecting material for her biography of Wolfe, she found among his manuscripts the typescript of the Purdue speech, with the exception of seven pages that he had taken out and worked into the manuscript of *You Can't Go Home Again*. The biography shows what a high value she placed on the document. She depended heavily on it along with other strictly autobiographical writings such as *The Story of a Novel,* the letters, and the pocket notebooks. She quoted from it frequently, and she cited it as evidence that in "the last year of his life he had found himself: he reached maturity, outgrew his need for a father-substitute, and lost his intense preoccupation with himself in a love for all of mankind."[8]

---

[7] Letter to Elizabeth Nowell, May 23, 1938, in *Letters,* p. 766.

[8] *Thomas Wolfe: A Biography* (New York: Doubleday, 1960), p. 16.

The Purdue Speech

Editors' Note on the Reading Text

The reading text of the speech is based on the original 63-page typescript. All of this but seven pages—18 through 24—is in the North Carolina Collection in the library of the University of North Carolina, where Wolfe's family deposited it along with other papers. The same pages are missing in the photostatic copy of the speech that the late Elizabeth Nowell had made several years ago when she was collecting material for her biography of Wolfe; her copy is now in the Thomas Wolfe Collection of William B. Wisdom in the Houghton Library, Harvard University.

Early in 1962 when we obtained permission to publish the speech, our first inquiries as to the whereabouts of the missing pages brought only disappointment. But then it occurred to us that since Wolfe had revised certain passages of the speech and used them in the closing chapters of *You Can't Go Home Again,* he might simply have lifted several pages out of the speech and worked them, in revised form, into the manuscript of the novel. We asked Mr. W. H. Bond, Curator of Manuscripts of the Houghton Library, whether he or one of his staff would hastily check the manuscript of the last four chapters of *You Can't Go Home Again* to see whether any of those sheets had originally been numbered between 18 and 24 inclusive. Following this procedure, Mr. Bond put us very much in his debt by finding four of the missing pages. Mr. Braswell later found the remaining three.

Problems arose, however, in establishing the text for publication. Though we now had the complete typescript, not all the pages were intact. The cheap yellow paper on which the dictation had been typed was too flimsy to endure much handling, and edges of three pages had been torn or worn away, with the resultant loss of about 35 or 40 words. Such hiatuses are here simply recorded, with no conjectures as to what is missing.

Wolfe was fortunate in having a secretary very proficient at taking dictation directly at the typewriter, but the system of communication could hardly have been expected to result in a letter-perfect transcription of the author's words. A few corrections by Wolfe indicate that he had not enunciated certain words clearly enough to be understood: he had said, for instance, "blocks of granite," not "box of granites," "the Romney marshes," not "the rumbling marshes," "flowing," not "floating." Corrections of this nature, together with Wolfe's and his secretary's corrections of typographical errors and misspellings, were of course incorporated into the reading text. Wolfe's changes in paragraphing and punctuation were also introduced.

But if the manuscript was to be published as a speech, not all the changes in wording could be accepted. Revisions which were obviously designed to transform passages into material for the novel were rejected, but changes in wording which could be regarded as simply stylistic were in almost all cases incorporated into the speech. In rare instances the original phrasing was retained because it seemed more suitable for oral delivery—more likely what Wolfe would have *spoken*.

In addition, we ourselves made a few changes which seemed editorially desirable. We silently corrected a few typographical errors and misspellings that had been overlooked, italicized the names of periodicals, and capitalized or reduced letters to lower case in accordance with standard usage. Because the speech was not *written* by the author but *dictated*, we did not look upon the original punctuation as sacrosanct. Wolfe had such high regard for his secretary's ability to punctuate that he left the punctuating to her, and indeed she was excellent at it. But the necessity of punctuating someone else's prose instantly by ear—especially Wolfe's, when he was momentarily in such a "fine frenzy" that the clauses rolled on and on—could result in occasional punctuation that might justifiably be altered for the sake of readier comprehension. Our changes in the punctuation are recorded in the Textual Notes at the end of the Reading Text. By referring to the Textual Notes, one can, in all essentials, reconstruct the original typescript.

The numbers in square brackets in the Reading Text refer to leaves of Wolfe's original typescript.

Writing and Living*

I am going to talk shop to you, because my own experience has been that if people have anything at all interesting to say it is likely to be concerned with shop, and because anything I can say to you will have to be concerned with shop. I am coming to you from the shop—my own—where I have been at work for many months. I don't think it matters much where your shop is, as long as you can get your work done in it. For seven or eight months past mine has been in New York City, in an old hotel. I suppose there are better shops and better places to have a shop than the place where I have been; but it has served its purpose very well. In the first place, the old hotel has tremendous rooms, high ceilings, loads of floor space to walk back and forth in—something that more smartly appointed new hotels do not always have. In the second place, the old hotel is not, as hotels in New York go, an expensive one. And in the third place, although I frankly do not believe that hotels are a most desirable permanent place of residence, in New York they do have this advantage: one doesn't have to take a lease—and if one is a writer, with income insecure, and the desire occasionally to travel, that is a big advantage.

Now, I am going to tell you something more about my shop, because for me, at any rate, it is important. I have a big room where I work, and another room where I sleep: I'd like to emphasize the fact of space, because I think almost [2] every capitalistic notion I have begins with space. I can do without a lot of things that many people not only would be uncomfortable without, but think essential. My luxury—and by an ironic paradox, in America of all places,

---

where there is so much space, it has really come to be a luxury—is space. I like to have a big place to work in, and if I don't have it I am uncomfortable. I've tried to describe and emphasize all these apparently trifling physical things to you, because they have been so important to me. I am a writer. And no matter what you may have heard about writers, my own experience has been that a writer is first and foremost a working man. This may surprise you. It does surprise most people. For example, it has always surprised my mother, who is an admirable old woman, seventy-eight years old, who has worked all her life, as hard as any person I've ever known, and who is today as alert, vigorous, active as any person of that age you know. But my mother, like so many other people, has never been able to get it into her head that writing is work. When I was home last summer, she said to me: "Now, boy, if you can get paid for doing the kind of thing you do, you're mighty lucky—for all the rest of your people had to *work* for a living!" I keep reminding her that writing is also work— as hard work, I think, as anyone can do—I keep insisting on the fact; and my mother amiably keeps agreeing. But also she keeps forgetting—and in unguarded moments, I often get flashes of what is really going on in what the psychologists call her subconscious. And apparently, it is something like this: writing is a kind [3] of stunt, a kind of trick which some people are born with—like being a sword-swallower or a left-handed baseball pitcher—and if one is fortunate enough to be born with this trick, or gift, he can, without much effort to himself, be paid for it. I don't believe my mother's views upon the subject are at all extraordinary: in fact, I should say they represented, unconsciously at least, the views of a majority of people everywhere. I know my mother would certainly be surprised, and possibly astonished, if I told her that I thought I was a working man—by this, I mean a man who does actual hard physical labor—in very much the same way as my father was, who was a stone-cutter; and if I told her that I looked upon the big room in which I work—with its crates of manuscript—its worktables—its floor space—in very much the same way as my father looked upon his shop in which he had his tombstones, his big trestles, his mallets and chisels, and his blocks of granite—my mother would smile, but would consider my proposition as another fantastic flight of the imagination. And yet, it seems to me, it is not fantastic. I am, or would like to be, a writer. And my own experience has been that a writer is, in every sense —particularly the physical one—a working man. And a writer, like other men who work, has a shop. And I am coming to you from the shop. And therefore, I am going to talk shop—because, it seems to me, it is likely to be the thing I can talk best, and that will be of greatest interest to you.

I wish I could tell you how to write stories in such [4] a way that you could sell them for high prices to well-paying magazines. But the plain, bitter truth is that I can't tell you how, because I don't know how myself. I wish I could tell you how to write novels so that you could get them accepted by good publishers and enjoy a tremendous sale. But the plain and bitter truth again is that I can't tell you, because I don't know how myself. In fact, I don't think I even know for certain what a story or a novel is—a fact with which many of my critics would enthusiastically agree. I am constantly being fascinated and tempted by those glittering advertisements one sees so often in magazines today, showing a vigorous and keen-faced gentleman shooting his index finger out at you and saying: *"You* can be a writer too!"—and then going on to tell you how Chester T. Snodgrass of Bloomington took his course last year and found out about it in ten easy lessons in such a way that he *tripled* his income. Well, I'd not only like most earnestly to triple my income, but I should like most desperately to find out about it. And someday, I think, I am going to write that keen-faced gentleman with the index finger and enroll. But help of that sort, I regret to say, I cannot give you tonight, for help of that sort is not in me. A year ago, in fact, my agent called me up and in a trembling voice informed me that we had just sold a story to the *Saturday*

Evening Post.[1] The whole world reeled around us for a moment; then we became exultant. Our fortunes were made. It all looked so easy—we were on the line. The news leaked out, and friends would say to me: "I hear you've broken into the *Saturday Evening Post*," to which [5] I would nod complacently, as if after all this was no more than was to be expected; and presently people were saying, "Well, I see you're a *Post* writer now—" at which I began to look and feel quite smug. My agent told me that the *Post* was so much interested in the story that one of its representatives had exacted from her a promise that she would not show the next story I wrote to anyone else before she had shown it to the *Post;* and we graciously consented to give them the first chance. Well, the upshot of it was, when I sat down and wrote another story, which we both gloatingly agreed was not only much better than the first story but had in it all the desirable elements that we thought a *Post* story should have—dialogue, characterization, and swift action; as for action we thought we had touched the peak, for I had the whole Battle of Chickamauga in. We debated whether we should let them have it for the same price as the first one, or whether the time had not now arrived—since I was an established *Post* writer—to demand Clarence Budington Kelland fees. We finally agreed that we would not be too severe, but would play them along diplomatically at first, and ask for only a thousand dollar raise or so. We thought it best not to hurry matters, and we agreed that it would probably be two or three weeks before we had their offer anyway. Well, we had their offer in six days—which was an offer of a flat rejection, with pained regrets that the story was not a *Post* story, and was lacking on the side of action. It was a stern blow, but we both recovered [6] rapidly: the agent pointed out that there was still *Redbook, Collier's, Cosmopolitan,* and so on, in the high-paying class, and that on the whole it would be better to let *Cosmopolitan* or one of the other big magazines have it anyhow, so that it would get my

---

1 "The Child by Tiger" appeared in *Saturday Evening Post,* September 11, 1937.

name around more to the great public. Well, the story came bouncing back from one big magazine after another with the regularity of a tennis ball: we decided then to try "the quality group"—*Harper's, Scribner's,* and so forth—because by this time we had decided the story was a "quality" story anyway. No matter what it was, it kept bouncing back; and after my valiant agent had tried all of them—eight months later—we landed! We sold that story! We landed in the *Yale Review!*[2] Now the *Yale Review* is an excellent publication—an admirable one—and anyone ought to be proud to be in it. But the difference, among other things, between being in the *Saturday Evening Post* and in the *Yale Review* is fourteen hundred dollars. I could have had a trip to Europe on the *Saturday Evening Post,* but all I got out of the *Yale Review* was an overcoat. I needed an overcoat very badly, and I spent all of my *Yale Review* check on the overcoat, and I got a good one. It was an English Burberry, solid wool and very thick, and it cost one hundred dollars. And then, just when I got the overcoat, we had no winter. It didn't go below freezing the rest of the time. Anyway, I've still got the overcoat.

But you see, if you expected to get someone out here [7] who could tell you how to write a story, and how and where to sell it to a high-paying magazine, you've come to the wrong man. You should have got that keen-faced fellow with the index finger who can tell you how. The most I can promise you is that if you ask me how to write a story that will get into the *Saturday Evening Post,* I will tell you how, and then you will wind up in the *Yale Review.* Perhaps this has its value, too; for it has occurred to me that the next time I want to sell a story to the *Saturday Evening Post,* I shall start out by writing it for the *Yale Review.*

I am thirty-seven years old, and for the past ten years, at least, I have been writing for publication. For the last nine years all my income, in one way or another, has been derived from writing. I think I can truthfully say that I have not only lived for writing, but I have also written to live. It's all I had to live on: I had no other source of

---

2 "Chickamauga" was published in *Yale Review,* Winter, 1938.

income—if I was going to keep on writing, I had to live
by it. I had to support myself. And yet, I can also truthfully say that, so far as I know, I have never written a word,
a sentence, or a paragraph, with the immediate objective of
making money out of it. Please don't think I'm being
snooty. I wish to God I did know how to go about de-
liberately coining words and sentences and paragraphs into
immediate and productive cash. I'd love it. That's why
I'm so fascinated by the keen-faced gentleman of the index
finger—his talk of "publics," "slants," and "writing for your
market," fascinates me. But, thus far, it is all Chinese to
me. I don't know how to go about it.

I can also say this truthfully. In the last few years [8]
I have rejected a number of offers that would have given
me a great deal more money than I have ever had. I
understand that my name as a writer is fairly well known,
and one of my books, at least, two or three years ago, got
pretty prominently into the bestseller list. But I counted
up my total earnings, over the past ten years, since I began
to write professionally, the other day, and found that they
did not total forty thousand dollars. That's a lot of money
—a lot more than most writers ever earn—and I certainly
am not disappointed or depressed about it. But, on at
least one occasion, I could have earned more than that
total sum in one year's time if I had accepted employment
that was offered me in Hollywood.[3] I didn't take it. Why?
I hasten to assure you that it was not because I was being
noble. I have listened to writers who had a book published shudder with horror at the very mention of Hollywood—some of them have even asked me if I would even
listen to an offer from Hollywood—if I could possibly sub-
mit my artistic conscience to the prostitution of allowing
anything I'd written to be bought in Hollywood, made into
a moving picture by Hollywood. My answer to this has

---

[3] Sam Marks, the story editor for Metro-Goldwyn-Mayer, told Elizabeth Nowell that since the offer of a position to Wolfe in 1935 and his de-
clining of it had both been oral, there was no record of it; but according
to Marks's recollection, "it was either on a week-to-week basis at $1000 to
$1500 a week, or on a yearly basis at $30,000 to $50,000" (*The Letters of
Thomas Wolfe*, p. 488, n. 2).

always been an enthusiastic and fervent *yes*. If Hollywood wants to prostitute me by buying one of my books for the movies, I am not only willing but eager for the seducers to make their first dastardly appeal. In fact, my position in the matter is very much that of the Belgian virgin the night the Germans took the town: "When do the atrocities begin?"

But when I got an offer to go there and work, [9] I did not take it, although it would have paid me more money than I had ever earned from writing in my whole life before; and I repeat again I have never felt noble about it. I did not go because I did not want to go. I wanted to write: I had work to do, I had writing, and still have, and I think will always have, that I wanted to get done. It meant more and it means more to me than anything else I could do. And I think that is the reason I am a writer.

Which brings us, it seems to me, to a somewhat deeper and more fundamental level—doesn't it? I have told you that I had to write to live—that if I go on writing, I must supply the sheer physical necessities of life out of the writing that I do. In one way or another, I have got to be paid for it; because I have no other money on which to live—and if writing as a means of support fails me, then I shall have to turn to other means that do not. And yet, even if that happened, I believe that, in some way, I would contrive to get my writing done. Because, from what I have told you, you will see that it has been in my life not only a physical and economic necessity; it has been, much more than that, a spiritual one. Why? That is what, with your tolerant permission, I'm going to try to tell you to-night; for it seems to me that if I can tell you anything at all that will be of any value or interest to you, it will in some way be tied up with this.

And it seems to me that if I can say to you what I want to say, it may be important, also, in a larger sense. [10] I mean a sense larger than the mere facts of personal auto-biography, which are relatively unimportant; a sense larger than the mere fact or chance or accident that I am a writer, or some of you will be lawyers, doctors, engineers,

or business men. I think that if I can say the thing, it
may be of some importance and some value to you because
it will represent the experience not only of one man, but,
in a certain measure, the experience of every man; because
if I can tell you honestly and truthfully about my own
work, about the changes and developments that have come
about in it, I can also tell you something about the changes
and developments that have come about in me—about my
own connection with the world, about what I think and
feel and believe about my work, and about the world, for
if the work a man does is living work—work in which his
mind, his spirit, and his life are centered—then it seems
to me his work may also be a window through which one
looks at the whole world. And writing *is* my work, it *is* my
life—just as law and engineering may be yours—and because it is, everything I know and think and now believe
is somehow vitally connected with this work I do.[4]

Twenty years ago, when I was seventeen years old, and
a student at Chapel Hill—which is the University in my
native state of North Carolina—I was very fond, along with
many of my fellows, of talking about my "philosophy of
life." We were very earnest about it. It seems to me that
we were always asking one [*hiatus*] our philosophy of life.
I'm not sure now what [*hiatus*] time, except that I am
sure [11] I had one. We were deep in philosophy at Chapel
Hill—we juggled about such formidable terms as "concepts," "moments of negation," and so on, in a way that
would have made Spinoza blush; and if I do say so, I was
no slouch at it myself. It would surprise many people today to know that at the age of seventeen I had an a-1 rating
as philosopher—"concepts" held no terrors for my young
life; I could lead with a "concept" and counter with a
"moment of negation" in a way that would even put Joe
Louis to shame: I could split a hair with the best of them,
and now that I have gone in definitely for boasting, I made
a *one* in Logic, and it was said it was the only *one* that had
been given in that course for twenty years. So you see,

---

4 Many pages of the typescript from this point on were revised and
used in *You Can't Go Home Again*. See Appendix I.

when it comes to speaking of philosophy, there is one before you who is privileged to speak.

I don't know how it goes with students of this day and generation here in Indiana, but I know that to the students twenty years ago at Chapel Hill, "philosophy" was a most important thing. We stayed up nights and talked about it. We discussed the idea of God most earnestly: truth, goodness, beauty were our meat. We had ideas about these things, and, believe me, I do not laugh at them today: we were young, we were impassioned, and it was not bad. One of the more memorable events of my college career occurred one day at noon, when I was coming up a campus path and encountered coming toward me one of my colleagues whom I shall call B. C. Jones—largely because that happens to be his name.[5] [12] B. C. Jones was also a philosopher, and the moment that I saw him coming towards me I knew that B. C. Jones was in the throes. B. C. was red-haired, gaunt and angular, he had red eyebrows and red eyelids—he had come from a family of primitive Baptists before he came to Chapel Hill—and now as he came toward me, everything about him, hair, eyebrows, eyelids, eyes, freckles, and even the knuckles of his large and bony hands, were excessively and terrifically red.

He was coming up from Battle Park, which was a noble wood, in which we held initiations and in which we took our Sunday strolls. It was also the place where we went alone when we were struggling with the problems of philosophy. It was where we went when we were going through what was known as "the wilderness experience," and it was the place from which triumphantly, when "the wilderness experience" was done, we emerged. B. C. was

---

[5] Baxter Columbus Jones, the friend referred to here, became an attorney in Bryson City, North Carolina. He served in the state legislature, and at the time of his death, in 1948, was the prosecuting attorney for the 20th judicial district. He was an active worker in the Baptist Church.

In a letter to the editors his wife says that he admired Wolfe and spoke of him often, saying he was "the most unusual man he knew, and in a way the most brilliant." She thinks he did not know that Wolfe had used him fictionally in chapter 45 of *You Can't Go Home Again*. So far as she was aware, he did not read that book, but he did read *Look Homeward, Angel*.

emerging now: he had been there, he told me, for the past eighteen hours. His "wilderness experience" had been a good one—he came bounding toward me like a kangaroo, leaping into the air in intervals, and the first and only words he said were: "I've had a Concept!" And then he passed—he left me stunned and fastened to an ancient tree, as B. C. went on down the path, high-bounding, kangaroo-like, every step or two, to carry the great news to the host.

And yet, I do not laugh at it. We were young men in those days, but we were earnest and impassioned ones, and each of us had his philosophy. And all of us—this was the sum and root of it—had his "Philosopher." He was a noble and a venerable man—one of those great figures that almost every college had some [13] twenty years ago, and that I hope they still have.[6] For fifty years he had been a dominant and leading figure in the life of the whole state: in his teaching he was, I think, what is known as a Hegelian— I know the process of his scholastic reasoning was intricate —and came up out of ancient Greece through a great series of "developments" to Hegel—and *after* Hegel—he did not supply the answer, but *after* Hegel was our Old Man.

Looking back, all that does not seem important now— our philosopher's "philosophy." Looking back, it seems at best a tortuous and patched-up scheme. But what was most important was the man himself: he was a great teacher, and what he did for us, what he had done for people in that state for fifty years, was not to give them his "philosophy"—but to communicate to them his own alertness, his originality, his power to think.

To us, he was a vital force, because he supplied to many of us, for the first time in our lives, the inspiration of a questioning intelligence. He taught us not to be afraid to think, to question; to examine critically the most ven-

---

[6] Horace Williams, Wolfe's professor of philosophy at the University of North Carolina, appears as Vergil Weldon in *Look Homeward, Angel*, chapter 38, and as Plato Grant in *You Can't Go Home Again*, chapter 45. There is an interesting assessment of Williams as a philosopher and as a personality in Richard S. Kennedy, *The Window of Memory: The Literary Career of Thomas Wolfe* (Chapel Hill: University of North Carolina Press, 1962), pp. 49-53.

erable of our native superstitions, our local prejudices, to look hide-bound conventions in the eye and challenge them. In these ways, he was a powerful and moving figure. Throughout the state, the bigot hated him; but his own students worshipped him to idolatry. And the seed he planted grew—the deposit of his teaching stayed—even when Hegel, concepts, moments of negation, had all gone, or had merged back into the confused and tortuous pattern from which they were derived. [14]

About this time, I began to write. I was editor of the college paper—which, in my day, and under my direction, always did have, at least, a certain archaeological interest —since it was interesting to examine in this week's edition the ruins and relics of last month's news. But in addition to this, I wrote some stories and some poems for the magazine of which I was also a member of the editorial staff.[7]

The War was going on then; I was too young to be in service, and I suppose my first attempts creatively may be traced to the direct and patriotic inspiration of the War. I remember one, in particular—a poem, I believe my first, which was aimed directly at the luckless head of Kaiser Bill. The poem was called defiantly "The Challenge," and I remember it was written in the style, and according to the meter, of "The Present Crisis," by James Russell Lowell.

I remember further that it took a high tone from the very beginning: the poet, it is said, is the prophet and the bard—the awakened tongue of all his folk—and I was all of that. In the name of embattled democracy, I let the Kaiser have the works, and I remember two lines in particular that seemed to me to have a very ringing tone— "Thou hast given us the challenge—pay, thou dog, the cost, and go!" I remember these lines so well because they were the occasion of an editorial argument at the time: the more conservative element on the editorial staff felt that the words "thou dog" were too [15] strong—not that the Kaiser didn't deserve it, but that they jarred

---

[7] He was editor-in-chief of the college paper, *Tar Heel*, in his senior year. As a junior he was one of five assistant editors of *Carolina Magazine*, and as a senior, the assistant editor-in-chief.

rudely upon the high moral elevation of the poem, and upon the literary quality of the Carolinian magazine. Above my own vigorous protest, they were deleted.[8]

I also remember writing another poem that year, which was the spring of 1918, about a peasant in a Flanders field who ploughed up a skull, and then went on quietly about his work, while the great guns blasted far away.[9] I also remember a short story—my first—which was called "A Cullenden of Virginia"—which was about the recreant son of an old family who recovers his courage, and vindicates his tarnished honor in the last charge over the top that takes his life.[10] These, so far as I can recall them, were my first creative efforts; it will be seen what an important part the last war played in them.

I mention all this just to indicate what has happened to me in the last twenty years, and because of its reference also to a charge that has sometimes been made by some of my friends. One of them,[11] for example, not more than three or four years my senior, is very fixed in his assertion of what he calls "the lost generation"—a generation of which he has been quite vociferously a member, and in which he has tried enthusiastically to include me. "You belong to it, too," he used to say. "You came along at the same time. You can't get away from it. You're a part of it whether you want to be or not"—to which my vulgar response would be: "Don't you you-hoo me!"

If my friend *wants* to belong to the Lost Generation— and it really is astonishing with what fond eagerness those people [16] hug the ghost of desolation to their breast—

---

8 The line referred to appears in the following couplet in the magazine for March, 1918: "We have taken up the gauntlet,—we will answer blow for blow,/ You have sent your blood and iron, pay thou then the cost, and go." "The Challenge" was not the first but the third poem Wolfe published in the college magazine.

9 In "A Field in Flanders," in the November 1917 issue of the magazine, the ploughing peasant does not actually appear but is only alluded to; the third and last stanza reads: "And to the right a ruined village burns,/ And to the left a wood its secrets hold,/ But in the gutted field the plowshare turns/ A grinning skull which sneers its message bold."

10 In *Carolina Magazine,* March 1918.

11 Scott Fitzgerald.

that's *his* affair. But he can't have me. If I have been elected, it has been against my will; and I hereby resign. I don't feel that I belong to a lost generation, and I have never felt so. Furthermore, I doubt very much the existence of a lost generation, except insofar as every generation, groping, must be lost. In fact, it has occurred to me recently, that if such a thing as a lost generation does exist in our own country, it is probably more those men of advanced middle age who spoke the language, and who know no other now, than the language that was spoken before 1929. These men indubitably are lost. But I am not of them, and I don't think I was ever part of any lost generation anywhere. The fact remains, however, I was lost. And the fact that I no longer feel so is what I am going to describe.

It is a little premature to start summing up one's life experience at the age of thirty-seven, and I certainly do not intend to do so here. But, although thirty-seven is not a very great age to have learned many things, it is time enough to have learned a few. Rather, it seems to me, by that time a man has lived long enough to look back over his life and see certain events and periods in a proportion and a perspective he could not have had at the time when they occurred. I think that has happened to me, and since each of those periods really represent to me a pretty marked change and development not only in my whole view about the work I do, but in my views on men and living and my own [17] relation to the world, I am going to tell about them now.

For the sake of convenience, I am going to begin at the time when I was about twenty years old, because I suppose that is about the age of many of you who are here tonight. Furthermore, it is a convenient date because it marks the date of my graduation from college, and the time when I was just beginning to hint timidly to myself that I might one day try to be professionally a writer. At that time, I did not dare go further than suggest this ambition to myself in the most hesitant and tentative fashion, and that period of hesitancy and reserve was to continue for at least six years before I ever dared to commit myself boldly and wholeheartedly to the proposition that I was a writer, and that henceforth *that* should be the work I did. Therefore, that first cycle, from about 1920 to 1926, is the one I am going to tell you about first.

Looking back, in an effort to see myself as I was in those days, I am afraid I was not a very friendly or agreeable young man. The plain truth of the matter is that I was carrying a chip on my shoulder, and I suppose I was daring the whole world to knock it off. The chip on my shoulder had, of course, to do with writing, and with the life I wanted to lead. And I suppose the reason I was outwardly so truculent at times, and inclined to be arrogant and take a very high tone with people who, it seemed to me, doubted my ability to do the thing I wanted to do, was that inwardly I was by no means so arrogantly sure that I could do it myself. It was a form of whistling to keep one's courage up. [18]

When I was graduated from college in 1920—I was then really just nineteen—I don't suppose it would have been possible to find a more confused or baffled person than I was. I had been sent to college in order to "prepare myself for life"—as the phrase went in those days—and it almost seemed that the total effect of my college training was to produce in me a state of utter unpreparedness. I had come from one of the most conservative parts of America, and from one of the more conservative elements of American life. So far as I know, all of my people until a generation before had been country people, whose living had been in one way or another derived out of the earth. Only within the past generation really had any of them "moved into town," and become business men—lumber dealers, contractors, and so forth. My father himself had been all his life a working man. He had done hard labor with his hands since the time he was twelve years old. He was a man of great natural ability and of a great deal of natural intelligence, and like many other men who have been deprived of the advantages of a formal education themselves, he was ambitious for his son, and wanted him to have one.

It is but natural that people of this kind should endow formal education with a kind of magic practicality: a college was a kind of magic door which opened to a man not only all the reserves of learning, but provided him with a kind of passport to success, a kind of magic key to the great material rewards of place or money that the world has to offer. Further, it is but natural that a man like this should seek for that success along one of the roads that had always been approved, and the road that he chose for me was law. I think he had himself cherished all his life an ambition to study law, and I think he had always regretted the accident of birth and of necessity that had prevented him from study- [19] ing it, and in a way I had been chosen as a kind of fulfillment of his own ambition. By 1920, it was already apparent that whatever I would be, I would never be a lawyer. By that time my father was old and sick, and had only a year or two more to live, and I knew that I had grievously disappointed him. For that reason alone, it was difficult to admit, even to myself, the stirrings of a desire to write; and the first admission that I made to myself was an evasive one. I told myself that I wanted to go into journalism, and the first work that I looked for was newspaper work. Looking back, the reason for this decision now seems transparently clear: I doubt very much that I had at that time the burning enthusiasm for newspaper work that I thought I had, but I convinced myself that I did have it, because newspaper work provided me with the only means I knew whereby I could, in some fashion, write, and earn a living.

To have confessed openly to my family at that time an outspoken desire to be "a writer" would have been impossible. And the reason why it would have been impossible was that in their consciousness—as well as in my own—"a writer" was a very remote kind of person, a romantic figure like Lord Byron, or Longfellow or—or—Irvin S. Cobb—who in some magical way was gifted with the power to write poems and stories and novels that were printed in books or in the pages of magazines like the *Saturday Evening Post*—and who, for all these reasons, was a very strange, mysterious kind of person, who lived a very strange, mysterious and glittering sort of life, and who came from some strange and mysterious and glittering sort of world, very far away from any life or any world that *we* had ever known.

That, I believe, represents pretty accurately the image we all had in our minds about "a writer"—and I believe it represents pretty accurately the image many people have today. I don't think my own family, for example, have [20] ever quite recovered from their own astonishment that I was, or was said to be, "a writer"; and if I had openly announced my intention of being one at the age of twenty, they would have been decidedly alarmed. And the reason they would have been alarmed—and later on were alarmed, when I did announce it—was that the whole thing would have seemed so fantastic and improbable to them. To be a writer was, in modern phrase, "nice work if you could get it"—if you could be a writer like Lord Byron or Longfellow or Irvin S. Cobb—but for one of the family, for a boy who had grown up in the town of Asheville, North Carolina, in Buncombe County—who had, it is true, *sold* the *Saturday Evening Post* on the streets of Asheville (if *that* was any sort of training for a writer)—now to openly assert he *was* one, or was going to be, bordered on the fringes of lunacy. It harkened back to the days of Uncle Greeley, who spent all his time learning to play the violin, and who borrowed fifty dollars from Uncle Jim one time to take a course in phrenology. I had always been told that there was a strong resemblance in appearance between myself and Uncle Greeley, and now I knew if I confessed my secret desires, the resemblance would seem to be a great deal more marked than ever.[12]

---

12 Wolfe is referring to his uncles Greeley and Jim Westall. Hayden Norwood, *The Marble Man's Wife* (New York: Charles Scribner's Sons, 1947), pp. 66-67, quotes Wolfe's mother as saying of Greeley: "He was kind of unbalanced. The teacher said, 'He knows more history than all the children in school.' But he couldn't learn the multiplication table. He didn't know a dollar from a five-dollar bill. But over at the old Asheville Female College, if they wanted to engage a musician to play they would call Greely [sic] in to listen to him first, and if Greely said he was all right, then they would hire him."

Well, it was a painful situation; it was, in many ways, an amusing one—it seems to me to be always such a human and American one, and it must be familiar to you all. At any rate, it was to shape the course of my life for years. That summer after graduation things turned out fortunately for me so that I got money whereby I could go to Harvard, and enroll in the graduate school for a year. And after that year was over, I managed to get money to go there for two years more, so that I was there for three years in all. Looking back upon that experience, I can see it now in a [21] clearer perspective. At the time, I don't think I knew clearly my reason for wanting to go to Harvard, except that I was still marking time, and couldn't clearly decide what I did want to do. But I argued strongly for the Harvard move on the ground that it would give me the chance to do graduate work and to get a graduate degree, both of which, I argued, would be useful to me no matter what I later did. The real reason was that I wanted to write, and this move, groping as it was, was nevertheless some further effort toward it. At Chapel Hill I had begun to write one-act plays under the direction of Professor Frederick Koch, who had come there while I was a student and established the organization which has now become widely known as The Carolina Playmakers. Several of these plays had been produced there by the Playmakers with some success, and now, at Harvard, it was not only natural but almost inevitable that I should seek for admission in the late Professor George Pierce Baker's Forty-seven Workshop. Thus, it turned out almost immediately that my graduate work at Harvard developed mainly into the business of writing plays—although it is true I took some other courses and picked up a Master's degree more or less incidentally, on the way.

From this point begins a newer development. At Harvard, for the first time in my life, I was thrown into the company of a group of sophisticated young people—at least, they seemed very sophisticated to me in those days. Instead of people like myself, who had felt within themselves the timid but unspoken flutterings of a desire to write, and to be a writer, here were people who openly asserted that they were. They not only openly asserted that they were, but they openly asserted that a great many other people that I had thought were [22] most dismally were not. I began to discover that when I made some hesitant effort to take a part in the brilliant conversation that flashed around me, I must be prepared for some very rude shocks.[13] For example, it was decidedly disconcerting to a Chapel Hill youth of twenty years, when he eagerly asked another Harvard youth of not much more than that: "Have you ever read Galsworthy's 'Strife'?"—to have that other youth raise his eyebrows slowly, exhale a slow column of cigarette smoke, shake his head slowly, and then say in an accent of resigned regret: "I'm sorry. I can't read him. I simply can't read him. Sorry—" with a kind of rising inflection, as if to say it was too bad, but that the situation simply could not be helped.

They were "sorry" about and for a great many other things and people—too, too many, it now seems as I look back, for it seems that there was hardly a leading figure writing for the theatre in those days who escaped their censure. Shaw, for example, was "amusing"—but he was not a dramatist, he had never learned how to write a play; O'Neill's reputation was grossly exaggerated—his dialogue was clumsy, and his characters stock types; Barrie was insufferable on account of his sentimentality; as for Pinero, Jones, and others of that ilk, their productions were already so dated that they were laughable—in fact, almost everyone was out of step, one gathered, except our own particular small groups of Jims. And our own particular small group of Jims were by no means sure of one another —it was usually a case of "everyone's wrong but thee and me, and even thee is for the most part wrong."

In a way, this super-criticality was a very good thing [23] for me. It taught me to be a good deal more critical and questioning about some of the most venerated names and reputations of the day, whose authority had been handed

---

[13] The passage that follows echoes the conversation of the sophisticated young men in Professor Hatcher's playwriting class in *Of Time and the River*, pp. 113-115.

down to me by the preceptors of the past, and which I had accepted in too unquestioning a way. But the trouble with it was that I was now tied up in the speeches of niggling and over-refined aestheticism, which, it seems to me, was not only pallid and precious, but too detached from life to provide the substance and the inspiration of high creative work.

It is interesting to look back now and to see just what it was we did believe ten or fifteen years ago—these bright young men and women of the time, who wanted to produce something of value to the arts. We talked a great deal about "art and beauty"—a great deal about "the artist"; it now seems to me that on the whole the total deposit of this was bad. It was bad because it gave to young people who were deficient in the vital materials and experiences of life, and in the living contacts which the artist ought to have with life, the language and the formulas of an unwholesome preciosity.

We talked about "the artist" a great deal too much; looking back, it seems to me that the creature we conceived in our imagination as "the artist" was a kind of aesthetic Frankenstein. Certainly, he was not a living man. And if the artist is not first and foremost a living man—and by this I mean a man of life, a man who belongs to life, who is connected with it, and who draws the sources of his strength from it—then what kind of man is he?

The artist we talked about was not this kind of man at all; indeed, if he had any existence at all, except the existence that we gave him in our conversations and in our imaginations, he must have been one of the most extraordinary and inhuman freaks that nature ever created. Instead of loving life and believing in life, this artist we talked about hated life and fled from it; for that, indeed, was the basic theme of many of the plays we wrote—[24] the theme of the sensitive and extraordinary person, the man of talent, the artist—crucified by life, misunderstood and scorned of men, pilloried and driven out by the narrow bigotry and mean provincialism of the town or village, betrayed and humiliated by the cheapness of his wife, finally, crushed, silenced, torn to pieces by the organized power of the mob.

This artist that we talked about so much, instead of being in union with life, was in disunion with it; instead of being near the world, was constantly in a state of flight from it. The world itself was like a beast of prey, and the artist like some stricken faun was trying to escape from it. The total result of this was inevitable: it was to develop a kind of philosophy, an aesthetic, of escapism. It tended to create in the person of the artist not only a special but a privileged character, who was not governed by the human laws that govern other men, who was not subject to the same desires, the same feelings, the same passions—who was, in short, a kind of beautiful disease in nature, like a pearl in an oyster.

The effect upon such a person as myself may also easily be deduced. Now, for the first time, I was provided with a kind of protective armor, a kind of glittering and sophisticated defense which would shield my own self-doubt, my inner misgivings, my lack of confidence in my own powers, my ability to accomplish what I wanted to do. The result was to make me arrogantly truculent where my own desires and purposes were concerned. I began to talk the jargon as the others did, to prate about "the artist," and to refer scornfully and contemptuously to "the bourgeoisie"—the Babbitts and the Philistines—by which, I am afraid, we meant almost anyone who did not belong to the very small and precious province we had fashioned for ourselves.

And, I am also afraid, that although we spoke [25] about "art," "the artist," and the work we wished to do in phrases of devotion and humility, there was not so much of either one in us as there was of snobbishness. We felt superior to other people, and we thought we were a rare breed; because one cannot really be superior without humility and tolerance and human understanding, and because one cannot be of a rare, higher breed without the talent and the power and the selfless immolation that true power and talent have, I think most of us deceived ourselves. We were not the rare and gifted people that we thought we were.

At any rate, so armed and so accoutered in the aesthetic garments that were fashionable at that time, I left Harvard and for several years I lived and worked in New York, supporting my body by teaching school in the daytime, and my soul by writing plays at night. During all this time I cannot say that things got better with me in my relation to my work and to the world. If anything, I think I became more truculent, for I was up against it now—I no longer had the soothing assurance of support from home, or the comforting agreements of sophisticated colleagues in the Harvard Yard. I was living all alone in the big city, earning my living, and trying to make my own way; and for the first time in my life, as far as my work and my ambitions were concerned, I was right up against it. In blunt phrase, I had to "put up or shut up"—not only to justify myself in the eyes of the world, but to justify myself in my own belief and faith and conviction and self-respect. That is certainly a hard time in the life of any young man —particularly of any young man who is trying to create. It certainly ought not to be ridiculed or laughed at, and I do not do so now; for the man is right up against the naked [26] facts of self and work—there is nothing beyond himself that can help him, his strength is in himself, and he has to pull it from himself; and if he cannot, there is no other hope for him. But it does explain also a good deal of the truculence and the arrogance of youth: its furious distemper, its conflict with the world. With me, the period was a time of stress and torment, for I had now committed myself utterly—there was no going back, no compromise, and my position was a desperate one. The result was I had pulled up my roots bodily, broken almost utterly away from my old life—from my family, my native town, my earlier associations—there was nothing for me now except myself and work. I suppose the almost religious belief I have in work may date from just this period; for I think it was the fact that I could work that saved me. The fact also was, I wanted to work, and felt that I had work to do; and I think that was also a fact of great importance—for, as I was to find, and as I already suspected, there are so many people who want to write, but who do not want to work; there are so many people who like to talk about being an artist without ever going to the tremendous expense of spirit, energy, and concentration that one has to go to if he is an artist. So that period, although still a confused and tormented one, and in some respects a mistaken one, was not by any means a wasted one; for in that time, I began to learn the great necessity of work.

My personal happiness did not grow any better; if anything it grew worse, because for several years after I left college I knew nothing but failure and rejection. I was still trying to write plays—although it was largely chance and accident that had led me to writing [27] plays, I was now fanatically convinced that plays were all that I could ever write, were all I cared to write, were what I had been destined by nature to write—and that unless I could write them, and succeed with them, my whole life was lost. This was not only wrong—it was as fantastically wrong as anything could be: whatever other talents I had for playwriting—and I think I had some—the specific requirements of the theatre for condensation, limited characterization, and selected focus were really not especially for me. Even my plays at that time showed unmistakably the evidence of my real desire—for they abounded in scenes and characters, a great variety of places and of people, too great a variety, in fact, for the economic and commercial enterprise of the theatre profitably to produce. Something in me, very strong and powerful, was groping toward a more full, expansive, and abundant expression of the great theatre of life than the stage itself could physically compass: it was something that had to come out sooner or later, as a pent flood bursts above a dam—and in 1926 I found it—and another cycle had been passed, another period of development begun.

I was in Paris in the summer of that year and, the beginnings of my plan now working in me, I bought a tablet and began to jot notations down. I simply jotted down on the pages of this tablet—without plot or plan, and often without order—a sequence of the things that I wanted to put into a book. In the autumn of that year I went to London, and stayed there several months, and it was during this time that I began the actual composition of the first book I ever wrote. When I returned to America early in the following year, the beginning of the book was written. I continued with it in New York day by day, working meanwhile at the University where [28] I had been formerly employed. The first draft of the book was finally completed in 1928, and after vicissitudes and disappointments which I shall not attempt to tell of here, but which led me to believe at last that I had failed, and had even deluded myself for all these years with the notion that I was a writer, the manuscript was read by a publisher, who wrote me about it immediately—I was in Vienna at the time.[14] When I returned to America, I went to see the publisher, and after some discussion the book was accepted. For the next few months I worked upon rewriting and revision, and in the fall of 1929, the book was published, and another stage in my experience had been passed; and still another begun.

It has seemed to me for some time that there is a kind of significance in the fact that my first book appeared in October, 1929. For me, it seemed that in a way my life— my working life—had just begun; but in so many different ways I did not know about, or even suspect at that time, so many things that I believed in, or thought that I believed in, were ended. Many people see in the last great war a kind of great dividing line in their own lives—a kind of great tale of two worlds, a world before the War, and a world after the War; but in my own experience, if I had to write my own tale of two worlds, I think I should be more inclined to use 1929 as the dividing line. Certainly, that has been the most memorable division in my own life that I can now recall.

---

14 On October 22, 1928, Maxwell Perkins, head editor of Charles Scribner's Sons, wrote to Wolfe in Vienna about the possibility of publishing *Look Homeward, Angel*; see *Editor to Author: The Letters of Maxwell E. Perkins*, ed. John Hall Wheelock (New York: Charles Scribner's Sons, 1950), p. 61.

Before that, as we have seen, my experience as a man and as a writer had passed through certain well-defined stages, all of which were very familiar to the times and to the lives of many other young men of the times. The son of an average small town family, I had in the early Twenties embarked upon a writing career—had decided to be a writer—a fact which was not only in complete variance [29] with the lives of all my other people before me, but was also symptomatic of a marked social tendency of the time —the desire of thousands of young men everywhere to write. I had passed through progressive stages of change and of development which were also characteristic of the time: I had gone through the stage of aesthetic preciosity, of talking about "art" and "beauty," and about "the artist"; of scorning "the bourgeoisie," the Philistines and Babbitts, who were not only not artists, but who could never understand "the artist," but belonged to a completely different, separate world. From this, which was a time, I am afraid, in which I talked a great deal more about "beauty" and "art" than I created it, expended a great deal more time in scorning and in ridiculing "the bourgeoisie" than in trying to find out who they were and what they were like—I passed into the period when I had to go to work, and where I learned for the first time what work —hard, creative work—was like, and where at last I began to spend more time in an effort to create "art" and "beauty" than in talking about it. And now finally, I had reached the stage of first accomplishment—where at last I had accomplished something, got it completed, accepted, printed, and put between the covers of a book, where for the first time the general public, if it so desired, could look at it.

This is certainly a definite and closely linked chain of clear development, and for me it marked the end of one great cycle. Although perhaps I did not know much in 1929, I did know a good deal more than I knew in 1920. I knew, first of all, that writing was hard work—desperately hard work—and whoever accomplishes a good piece of writing must work hard and constantly, with exhausting concentration, and not depend upon sporadic flashes of casual [30] inspiration to do the job for him. I knew furthermore, and finally, that I could write—that I was able to see a job through to the end, and able to get it published by a good publisher. It is not necessary to point out what an inestimable comfort this knowledge was to me, for it had served to establish some confidence in my own abilities which I had never had before, and to restore my self-respect and my belief in myself and in what I wanted to do, which had been shaken by years of failure and frustration. I was certainly a wiser man in 1929 than I was in 1920, and I think I was also a stronger and surer one. I no longer had so big a chip upon my shoulder, I was no longer so truculent and occasionally arrogant in my relations to other people, because I no longer felt such inner need to prove to myself that I could do what I wanted to do. But I suppose a good deal of the old foolishness still remained: I would have smiled in 1929 at some of the aesthetic snobberies and preciosities of the young men at Harvard in 1923, but if anyone had asked me why I wrote, why I wanted to be a writer and continue to write books, I would have said some of the same things that I had said years before: I would have talked about "the artist," and I suppose I might still have had a romantic and fanciful notion of him, and of his relations to society. I am afraid I might also have talked a good deal about "art" and "beauty"—perhaps I shouldn't have been so hard on "the Babbitts and the Philistines," and as arrogantly scornful of "the bourgeoisie" as I had been in 1923—but I would have still looked down on them from a kind of aesthetic altitude and felt that they belonged to a separate order of things, in a different world. I was a lot closer to life, to people, to the world around me, to America in 1929, than I had ever been before; although I was still too detached from [31] it, not nearly close enough. But the experience of the last few years—the experience of work—the necessity of work—the fact that I really had worked had now brought me much closer to life, much closer to an understanding of the lives of people, as I think work always does. And for the last three years, before the publication of my first book, the work I had been doing had taught me much—that work, in substance, had demanded a kind of spiritual and emotional excavation of the deepest and intensest sort into the life I had known and of which I had been a part—the life of my home town, of my family, of the people I had come from—of the whole structure and frame of things that had produced me. I knew more about all of this than I had ever known before, but, as I was to discover, I did not know enough. For one thing, the book still showed unmistakably the evidence of the stages I had gone through, the periods of development, the special aesthetic faiths and creeds of the time. It is what is called an autobiographical novel—a definition with which I have never agreed, simply because it seems to me every novel, every piece of creative writing that anyone can do, is autobiographical. Nevertheless, it is true that this book was autobiographical in the personal and special sense: it was possible, for example, to identify the life of the hero with the life of the author—to suspect that a great many of the characters and incidents in the book were drawn pretty closely and directly from the writer's own experience. And, although I have not read the book for years, I believe that in this sense of the word—in this special autobiographical sense—was the book's greatest weakness: I believe the character of the hero was the weakest and least convincing one in the whole book, because he had been derived not only from experience but colored a good deal [32] by the romantic aestheticism of the period. He was, in short, "the artist" in pretty much the Harvard Forty-seven Workshop sense of the word—the wounded sensitive, the extraordinary creature in conflict with his environment, with the Babbitt, the Philistine, the small town, the family. I know that I was not satisfied with this character even at the time: he seemed to me to be uneasy and self-conscious, probably because I was myself uneasy and self-conscious about him. In this sense, therefore, the book followed a familiar pattern—a pattern made familiar by Joyce in *A Portrait of the Artist as a Young Man,* and later in

Ulysses—a book which at that time strongly influenced my own work. But I think the book also had been conceived and created with some of the blazing intensity of youth: although I did not know it at the time, in that sense of the word the book was a kind of passionate expletive—a fiery ejaculation hurled down upon a page of print because it had to come out, it had to be said. Here, too, my real education was beginning, for as yet I did not know these things. Again, the book had a rather extraordinary career: although it was on the whole well-reviewed and well-received throughout the rest of the country, and had, for a first book, a moderately good sale, in my own home town it was received with an outburst of fury and indignation that in my own experience has not been surpassed, and that I believe is even extraordinary in anyone's experience. Briefly, the people of the town read the book as if it had been the pages of the *World Almanac;* and seeing that some things were true, they became almost immediately convinced that everything was literally true and literally intended; and from this they became so outraged that they denounced me and my book individually and in the mass —from the pulpits, from the street corners, and from the public press; in letters signed, and in letters anonymous; and in threats that included tar and feathers, hanging, [33] gun-shot, and all other forms of sudden death. Their outrage and anger, although mistaken, were unmistakable: there is no doubt that from the moment of the book's publication, I became an exile from my native town. I could not have come back at that time, and it was seven years, in fact, before I wanted to come back, and did return.

This was bewildering and overwhelming: it was all different from what I had expected—so different from the reception that I had hoped to have in my home town that for a time my own sense of grief, disappointment and chagrin were very great; for one of the things it is hard to lose is the desire for the approbation and applause of one's own neighbors—the knowledge that one has succeeded in the estimation of the people of his own town. Moreover, it did do something to strengthen me in a further belief in what was perhaps the fundamental theme of the whole book—the story of the sensitive young man in conflict with his environment, driven out at last, forced to flee and escape from his own town. For now that had happened to me, and if that had been all that had happened, it might have embittered me into further belief and confirmation of my earlier error. Fortunately, there were other compensations: if I had been driven out at home, I had been accepted elsewhere; if my own towns-people had read my book with outrage and indignation, the larger public had read it as I had intended it to be read, as a book, as a work of fiction, as a product of the creative imagination which, if it had any value at all, had value because it was just as true of Portland, or Des Moines, of people everywhere, as it was of my own town.

So there I was in 1929, at the end of one route, at the beginning of another, at the end and the beginning of so many different things I then did not know or suspect, that looking back now, I seem to have been a guileless innocent. On the whole, my view of things was pretty [34] hopeful, pretty cheerful, for although I did have the desolating and rather desperate sense of exile, of having pulled up my roots completely as far as the old life was concerned, I had a feeling now of new beginning, too—of being launched at last, of having before me the happy prospect of an established and productive career. At that time, among the many other things I did not know, I did not know that for a man who wants to continue with the creative life, to keep on growing and developing, this cheerful idea of happy establishment, of continuing now as one has started, is nothing but a delusion and a snare. I did not know that if a man really has in him the desire and the capacity to create, the power of further growth and further development, there can be no such thing as an easy road. I did not know that so far from having found out about writing, I had really found out almost nothing: I had made a bare beginning, I had learned at best that I could do it. I had made a first and simple utterance; but I did not know that each succeeding one would not only be harder and more difficult than the last, but would be completely different—that with each new effort would come new desperation, the new, and old, sense of having to begin from the beginning all over again, of being face to face again with the old naked facts of self and work, of realizing again that there is no help anywhere save the help and strength that one can find within himself.

Again—and now I was moving to another deeper stage—I had not realized yet that the world changes, that the world is changing all the time, that the world, indeed, is in a constant and perpetual state of revolution—and that a man, a creative man most of all, if he is going to live and grow, must change with the world. I did not realize, in fact, even in 1929, that those images and [35] figures of my experience and training—the image of "the artist" and of "art," of "beauty" and of "love," of the wounded sensitive, driven out and fleeing away from the Philistines of the tribe—all of which had seemed so fixed and everlasting in the scheme of things, were really just the transient images of the times, a portion of the aesthetic belief and doctrine of the period. I did not realize that the year 1929, which was so important to me in such immediate personal ways concerning my own life and my immediate career, was to be a fatal and important year in so many other ways I did not even know about at that time, in so many ways affecting the life of the nation and of all the people in it, affecting human beliefs, that it seems now to mark a dividing line between two worlds. About the organized structure of society in 1929—its systems of finance economy, politics and government—and how they shaped and affected the lives of people, I knew almost nothing, and had never considered it a part of my interest to question or examine them. Certainly, if anyone should have suggested to me, in 1929, that it was not only a part of the purpose and function of an artist to examine them, but that if he continued to produce, his participation and examination would be inescapable, I should have denied the proposition utterly. I should have said that the purpose and the function of the artist was to create, to create what was true and beautiful, without reference to its social implications as regards the world around him; I think that I should probably have further said that the interest of the artist in such things as economics, politics, government, the organized structure of society, was not only outside the province of his life and work—to create the beautiful and true—but would probably be alien and injurious to it, if he allowed it to intrude [36] in what he did.

The fact that I no longer feel this way, and how and why, and by what degrees and stages I have come to feel differently, marks the last stage of my development at which I have now arrived, and I am going to try to tell you about it now.

When I went abroad, for a year's stay, early in May, 1930, some seven months after the publication of my first book, the great American depression was already well under way. And yet, my life was still so absorbed with matters of more personal and immediate interest to me that I had very little idea of what had happened. True, I was aware that there had been a "crash" in Wall Street—a whole series of them—for I had been in New York when they had occurred, and, in one way or another, a great many of the people that I knew were involved in them. In a general way, I was aware that almost everyone was involved, because I had become conscious in the past few years, while I was absorbed in my own work of creation, that there had been a general widespread change in lives of people everywhere, of no matter what walk or station. In later years, certain unforgettable memories would come back: I could remember a day in Vienna in October 1928, when the market was at its peak: a group of Americans, men and women of middle age sprawled out on the seats of a big sight-seeing bus, outside of a tourist agency, everyone of them absorbed in the stock page of the Paris edition of the New York *Herald Tribune*. And I remember going home to North Carolina, in the summer of 1927, I believe, and discovering with a sense of shock that a great many of my friends— young men of about my own age—were more feverishly in contact with one element of New York life than I was:

there was a stock ticker in a broker's office in one of the office buildings [37] in the town—something I had never known there before—and it seemed to have become a kind of rendezvous of many of the younger people, who were combining their speculation in the local real estate market—for the town itself was in the throes of a feverish boom —with speculation in the New York market. And everywhere around me there were flashes, picked up here and there, day after day, that indicated to me that something was happening to the whole country and to all its people that I had never known before: one would see taxi drivers buried in the latest stock reports; newsboys were familiar with the latest prices; at the city university where I taught, some of the instructors were speculating with their slender salaries. I caught the fever very strongly from some of my own friends. Two of them, young men whom I had known at Harvard, were now employed writing programs for the radio, and they were quite seriously involved in the market, as were most of their friends; and I remember one very well, a young man who had been an actor, and who was now a director in the radio, but whose main interest now had become his speculations in the market, which were said to have succeeded fabulously, and already to have mounted to a great fortune. I remember how, when the "crash" came, he was wiped out overnight; and then, he just bled very quietly to death—it only took a few days, but he started bleeding from his veins, and they could not stop it; the blood soaked out like water through a sponge until the man was dead; and I remember his funeral—or rather his funeral services—for everyone was very modern in those days, and wanted to avoid the protracted horror of a burial; so all his friends were called up and told that everything was going to be very casual and pleasant—that "Tony would like it better [38] that way"—and that "the services would be very short"; and they were—so short, in fact, they were over almost before one got seated; the preacher arose and spoke cheerfully for about five minutes, and said how happy Tony must be to know that all his friends were here, because his was such a bright and cheerful nature, etc.—and then it was all over, and everyone shook hands and filed out and no one even mentioned the fact that Tony was dead—and there was nothing unpleasant there to remind us that he was, because his body had been quietly cremated that morning. And I remember another man, a Wall Street broker, whose family I knew; they were the most fashionable people of my acquaintance, and now that my book was out, I was invited to dinner at the great apartment on Park Avenue; and there were brilliant and distinguished-looking men there, and the women were very beautiful and glittered, but the broker suddenly was all shriveled up: he had always been such a spruce and jolly-looking man, plump and ruddy with waxed moustache points like Otto Kahn's; now all this was gone except the moustache points. He had just collapsed like a balloon; even the plumpness and the ruddiness had gone out of his cheeks, until now they were withered like an old apple, and he sat there huddled by the fire in the living room of his great apartment, with all the brilliant and glittering people moving about him, an old man with a rug about his shoulders, with the maids bringing him things in glasses which he took: and you could just see something oozing out of him as he sat and shook and dwindled there before the fire.

Yes, I had seen all these things by the time I went abroad in 1930, but as yet it was their personal tragedy or drama, not their wider significance, of which I was aware. And looking back, [39] I cannot say that any of my intellectual or artistic contemporaries were any more aware of what had happened than I was. There was still a large expatriated colony of Americans in Paris: some of them had come back recently, and the burning intellectual issue of the day was classicism versus romanticism. In fact, on the night I sailed for Europe, which was May 9, 1930, this great issue was reaching its climactic apogee; for a group of our most brilliant moderns were meeting Professor Irving Babbitt in debate at Carnegie Hall—the future of culture was at stake, and that night the great issues that might determine the whole course that the arts must take were to be stated and defined.[15]

As for myself, I was thinking of another book, and of the fact that I had let some months elapse since the first one had appeared, and had been so immersed in the turmoil of my own emotions—the huge disturbance my first book had created at home—that I had done very little toward the second one; and I was conscious now of the fatal impingement of time: a sense of pressure, and the knowledge that I must get to work at once, make good use of my year abroad—I was going by the grace of Guggenheim[16]—and have a new book finished, if I could, by the time I came back. I suppose if I thought anything about the existing crisis in the nation's finance, I thought of it as a specialized and localized thing—something which largely affected a place called Wall Street and a special group of people who did business there. But I did not understand in what manifold and complex ways those strands were meshed into the whole web; I had been in New York and had seen the spectacular and dramatic flashes of explosion, but the dull thundering detonations that were later to come, the sight of the whole mass slowly detaching iself and rumbling down in dusty ruin was yet [40] to come. I did not know of it; I did not foresee it—Mr. Hoover was still around giving reassurances from time to time, and confident the worst was over. May, June, July—the early summer passed in Paris; and I worked. I saw a few Americans, two young women and their brothers who were on a jaunt; one of the men had grown a beard, and it had turned out fiery red, to everybody's huge amusement; they lived in a little, very cheap but very good, hotel on a square behind the Bibliotheque Nationale; the weather was lovely, and there were trees and a little fountain in the square; and I would

---

15 The New York *Times*, May 10, 1930, p. 4, reported: "Professor Irving Babbitt of Harvard, champion of the new humanism, invaded New York, the stronghold of his enemies, last night, when he engaged in a debate in Carnegie Hall with Carl Van Doren and Henry Seidel Canby." Van Doren took "a position diametrically opposed" to that of Babbitt while Canby defended "the midway point of view."

16 He had recently been awarded a Guggenheim Fellowship of $2,500.

go there almost every day for lunch; and one of the girls had learned to make deliciously cold and heady cocktails in an enormous silver shaker from a formula she had invented herself; and after this, we would all go down and have lunch on the sidewalk in front of the little restaurant downstairs; and amuse ourselves watching old, old men tottering back and forth with great loads of books across the endless tiers of the great Bibliotheque; and, what was most amusing, watch other men, both young and old, go in and out the doors of the sumptuous and celebrated brothel just to one side of the Bibliotheque which is known as the House of Nations; and after we had eaten, the man with the red beard would get out his accordion, which he had learned to play in a few weeks' time; and he would play it, and sometimes we would sing; and later on I would go back home to work, and the others would separate and go to various places; we would make arrangements to meet again that evening. It was a very pleasant summer.

Later on, in July and August and September, I was in Switzerland; and I had a room in a small but very clean hotel at Montreaux, and my room had a large stone balcony, and down below there was a lawn that was a sheet of velvet, and flowers seemed [41] to have been embroidered there, and all this stretched directly to the lake, which was fifty yards or so away, and of a blue incredible; and across the lake, on the French side, were the Alps that you had to look at twice before you believed they were there; and even then you didn't quite believe it; and it was very quiet, a few casual and intimate voices of people down below, and of the kitchen help; and every now and then the great, fast thrash of the paddles as the lake steamers, white and clean as swans, came into the landing down below, disgorged and took on, and then, with startling speed, were on their way again. Meanwhile, I worked upon my book, and occasionally I saw Scott Fitzgerald, who was living at Vevey, a mile or two away, and two or three times, when Swiss cooking got too dull, I would take an airplane and fly to France, where the cooking was not dull, to Dijon, or to Leon, even to Marseilles. So the summer passed. Late

in September, early autumn of that year, I was in the
Black Forest, in Freiburg. It is a lovely city, and the country all around is a haunted and enchanted one; I remember
being in a country inn towards sunset, and watching the
slant of light on mown fields, cool, darkening up the slopes
of the Black Forest; and I remember how some cows ran
through an arch and out upon a road, a straw-haired boy
of fourteen whacking them upon their stringy dung-spat-
tered behinds; I remember the dry, hard, wooden sound
their hooves made as they came into the road, and there
was everywhere around a clean pervasive smell of hay, of
stables and manure. I remember the people were excited,
for the time was approaching for the great Wahl—or na-
tional election—and I remember the excitement of election
day in Freiburg; and there were over twenty parties run-
ning; and keen interest in the Nazis and the Communists;
I remember that that year the Communists [42] got four
million votes.

Early in October, I was in England, saw my publisher,
and other people that I knew, and now for the first time I
heard the sound of the dull, the muffled detonations. For
the first time, I heard that there were breadlines in America, and that there had been riots, that already conditions
in some places were desperate; and I remember hearing my
publisher, a young man who, I think, had never liked
America very much, say grimly: "It's going to be bloody!
Bloody! They are cruel people over there—they'll let their
people die! It's going to be bloody, wait and see!"

Other people were excited and surprised. What was happening in America? they would ask me. For years they had
heard of America's fabulous prosperity, of high wages, of
carpenters and factory-hands who rode to work in motor
cars. And now, with explosive suddenness, they were reading that these same people were starving, were standing
in long queues along the streets to get a mug of coffee and
a crust of bread. How could this happen? they asked me,
and I, too, was dazed. Everything had happened so explo-
sively, and I had no answer, except suddenly it came to me
that things do happen with explosive suddenness in Amer-

ica: the way spring comes, for instance, exploding from the earth overnight, the way it goes just as suddenly, and summer is there. And now, it was not spring or summer: these were over, there was desolation, cold and bitter want at home.

One morning in November, I awoke to look out on dumb yellow fog, and to find that the ruin had come at last to my home town. That morning there was a small item in the *Daily Mail* announcing that the bank at home had failed; and knowing this meant ruin to many people that I knew, I cabled. Soon I had a letter, giving [43] fuller details of the bank's failure and the town's collapse—a failure and collapse that had been surpassed in magnitude in the nation's history, because the town is not a large one, but never in completeness or extent. The bank had gone down, carrying with it the government, the business, the commercial and industrial life of the whole town. As the details poured in, there was revealed a picture of catastrophe—a picture of the whole corrupted web, the huge honeycomb of speculation, paper, inflation and deceit—which, beginning as such things do, with some show of probability, with enthusiasm, and a measure of restraint, had mounted, mounted for ten years through all the successive stages of public drunkenness and hysteria. And now the whole thing was in ruins—not only the life of the town, but the lives of all its people: it was an appalling microcosmos of the whole breakdown—in feverish miniature, a picture of the whole boom that had swept the nation. And now, like the man I had known a year before in New York City, hundreds of people I had known all my life bled quietly to death. The whole town bled to death: dozens of people took their lives in those first weeks, dozens died from shock, from grief, from defeat, from disappointment and despair; and thousands more with all life taken from them were left to live. I sent money to those I could help, the winter passed, I worked upon my book, and early in the spring, in March, the following year, I went home.

The scene had changed: it was as if a bleak gray weather had come into the lives of everyone. Everywhere around one

now one heard of nothing but the tragedies of the so-called
depression. The change in intellectual life was also vast—
in many respects, it seemed to me, it was too sudden. Young
men of brilliant minds and talents who had been vigorously
debating the merits of classicism and romanticism [44] ten
months before, who had for years lived a life of disdainful
expatriation, had overnight, it seemed, become learned
economists. Their language and ideas were now not only
wholly new, but it was impossible to gather that they had
ever had any different ones. They spoke of the revolution-
ary movement as if they had been suckled at its breast,
since they were babes in arms; they were themselves deri-
sive of the little schools and cliques of obscure cults and
writings of which they had themselves been just ten months
before the most productive part. One such, whom I had
met a few months previous in Paris, and who had come
home with me on the boat, was indicative of the suddenness of these conversions: his own career had illustrated
aptly the dilettanteism of the time before. The descendant
of an enormously wealthy family, he had passed successively
through the stages of Greenwich Village, the Left Bank,
and little magazineism. He had run a bookshop for a while
and had endowed with his own funds one of the better
known obscure little magazines of the time. He had been
the hero—or the villain—of a celebrated novel of the Twenties, which had dealt with the lives and adventures of
young drunken people in Paris and in Spain.[17] And at the
time I met him, even at the very moment of our arrival
back in New York, he was neck-deep in the Palestine movement: he had just returned from there, he was writing
articles about it, his whole life and faith and energy was
now given to this cause. Within three weeks of my return
I heard from him again. He invited me to a party at his
place in Greenwich Village; and now again, the man's

---

17 When Hemingway's *The Sun Also Rises* appeared in 1926, the
character Robert Cohn was immediately recognized as based on Harold
Loeb, expatriot writer, little-magazine editor, and relative of the wealthy
Guggenheim family. In his autobiographical *The Way It Was* (New York:
Criterion Books, 1959), Loeb told his side of the story related in Heming-
way's novel.

horizon had all changed. When I came in, he asked me what I had been doing and I told him I had been writing. "Writing?" he said inquiringly, puffed meditatively [45] on his pipe a moment, and then smiling tolerantly, he said: "You writers." "What do you mean 'you writers'?" I demanded. His use of the pronoun was surprising, for only three weeks before he had certainly, by his own proclamation, been one himself. "I mean," he explained—"how can anyone possibly be interested in writing books when there are so many other things to do? Besides, how can you writers write about anything when you know nothing about economics?"

Yes, the effrontery of it was appalling, but it had happened. Within three weeks' time, the ex-Left Banker, little magazine-er, cafe-drinker, and Palestine movementer had become a world economist. He had fallen in apparently with an extraordinary character who called himself an engineer, and who said that the only hope of the world was for the engineers to take charge of it and plan it out anew along the lines of technical economy. By these means, with the potential wealth existing in our resources, in our inventions and discoveries, and in our means of production, it was possible for every man to live like a king in his own right—to have the equivalent of fifteen thousand dollars a year. Our new convert, however, had not only lapped all this up, he had improved upon it; and within four weeks he had his own book ready, which blandly set up a new world of economy, based on technical means, which promised everyone the equivalent of twenty thousand dollars a year.[18] So, he was off on a new track; but really, it seemed to me, very much the same track he had always been on.

The effrontery, and what seemed to me also to be the bland dishonesty, of these quick conversions disgusted and

---

[18] Written under the influence of Howard Scott, the technocrat, Loeb's *Life in a Technocracy: What It Might Be Like* (New York: Viking Press, 1933) projects a utopia in which a citizen would earn annually "20,000 x-ergs' worth of energy" by working only four hours four days a week (see p. 55). Without reading the book, Wolfe might have obtained such facts from an interview with Loeb, "Finds No Servants in a Technocracy," published in the New York *Times,* January 11, 1933, p. 17, or from certain reviews.

repelled me. But, it was nevertheless manifest that something in the structure in the life around us was seriously
amiss. I had seen the evidences [46] of collapse in the collapse of my own town; and now new evidences were coming to me day by day. For the first time in my life I began
to examine critically the life around me—to ask for the
reason behind the fact. For the first time, the assurances
of well-fed people began to look and sound spurious in the
face of suffering and starvation that one saw everywhere.
It was no longer enough, for example, to be told that "these
depressions have always been, and are bound to recur
from time to time"—that explained nothing; besides that, it
was in direct contradiction to the boast that some of the
most knowing of these people—a professor in the Harvard
Business School had been one of them—had made to me
only a year and a half before: that there would never again
be another depression, that the cycle of "prosperity" had
been permanently insured, that modern business and finance methods had now learned to control these things in
such a way that they could never happen. And now they
were not only happening, but they were happening to a
degree that they had never happened before; and the
vaunted system which had been able to prevent them was
now not only unable to prevent them, but lay itself in
ruins, with its chief directors calling for help. It was no
longer enough to be told, when one saw shabby and bat-
tered men begging for a cup of coffee or for ten cents, the
reason these people begged was because they wouldn't
work; it was no longer enough to be told that these people
would not take work even if it were offered them, because
this was no longer true, if it had ever been. More than
this, even with those shipwrecked men that one saw along
the Bowery, along the waterfront, in City Hall Park,
huddled in doorways or squatting in the foul congestion
of public latrines, sometimes stumbling blindly with the
poison of cheap drink, sometimes incoherent of tongue and
[47] addle-witted, it was no longer enough to be told that
these men were nothing but stumble-bums, that they would
only take the money that one gave them to buy more drink

with, that we had always had such people, that we always would. It was no longer enough to be told these things, because for the first time in my life I wanted to know, in the name of God, why? I was working furiously on a new book—really, a work of tremendous exploration and excavation—discovering, for the first time, the look of things, the feel of things, the size, shape, smell and taste of things, particularly here in America: it had all suddenly exploded into my consciousness with a kind of intensity and significance it had never had before—I was crystalizing for myself the whole material picture of the universe, of the world around me—the great job now was just to dig it up and get it down, get it down—somehow record it, transform it into the objective record of manuscript—even upon thousands and thousands of pages that would never be printed, that no reader would ever see, that would never be framed into the sequence of a narrative—but at any rate, now would be *there* at last upon the record—worth all the labor of the effort just so long as I could get it down, get it down.

And that enormous task of excavation, of exploration and discovering, went on for four years in Brooklyn, while slowly the structural lineaments of a book appeared. Meanwhile, through work, through the marvelous vitalizing power of work, through the intensity of my own effort, the world kept soaking in. It kept soaking in like light out of the dull gray weather, like sunlight in the month of May, like small fine moisture, like a steady rain. [48] Young men were writing manifestos in the higher magazines of Manhattan, but the weather of man's life, the substance and the structure of the world in which he lives, was soaking in on me in those years in Brooklyn, in those countless days and hours spent in my room, above my table, looking out the window, walking the endless jungle of the streets, talking to men all night in all-night coffee-shops, in subways, along the waterfront, upon the bridges, in South Brooklyn, upon trains, in the cinders of day coaches going west, in rooming houses in Washington, from my own people, and the story of their own ruin, which was the town's, from everything I'd ever seen or felt or known or heard about, now coming in upon me the way things must, not learned by a lightning stroke from Heaven, by a swift conversion from the Mount—but soaking in like cold gray weather, soaking in like cold gray rain, soaking in with my my own life and breath and work and blood and pulse, and the desperation of my own endeavor—to get it down, just get it down: a deeper furrow of the plow, a deeper bite of the drill, another depth, another level I had never touched before. And it was this:

My job was done in 1935—the job on which I had been busy for four years—and suddenly I knew that I was through with many things. I knew that I should never write, or want to write again, the kind of books that I had written before. I had wanted to follow the book I had completed with a book about a love affair, about a woman, and about a young man in the city: for two years I had poured my energy and talent into the composition of such a book, and now I had what I had, I knew what I knew—and I was done with it. It was really not farewell to love—but it was farewell to the way I had felt about it. Just as the individual conflict, the pain and suffering of a sensitive young man at odds with life, and with the forces of family in his native village, no longer [49] seemed so important to me as they had before, so did the individual ecstasies or heartbreaks of a love affair between a man and a woman not seem as memorable and as universal as they once had. It was not that I now despised these things, or thought that they were contemptible: I recognized their validity, and the important place they have always had and will continue to have in the lives of men, but my circle had widened, the range of my interest had increased immeasurably—those four years of work, of discovery, of exploration and of recording, of letting the weather of life and of humanity soak in upon my consciousness, had taken me out of the more narrow provinces of myself and of my work, of personal happiness or frustration, the vanity and the preoccupation of my view.

From this time on things mounted quickly to a head.

All of my life ever since childhood, I had wanted what all men want in youth: to be famous and to be loved. Now, I had had them both and—there is not time or need here for apology or equivocation—I can only say that, so far as I was concerned, they were not enough. And I think, if we speak truth, the same has been true of every man who ever lived and grew, and had the spark of life and growth in him. It has never been dangerous to admit that fame was not enough—it has, indeed, by one of the greatest poets who ever lived been called the "last infirmity of noble minds"—but it has been, for reasons that I cannot say, or at any rate, shall not mention here, been dangerous to admit the infirmity of love. And yet—or so it seems to me, as a simple product of what I have myself known—there may not have been a grown and a living man who has never known the knowledge that love brought to him; but there cannot be a grown and a living man who has not escaped the circle of its small tight whole. [50]

Perhaps, the image of it may suffice some people; perhaps, as in a drop of shining water, love may hold in microcosmos the reflection of the sun and the stars and the heavens and the whole universe of man; and mighty poets dead and gone have declared that this was true, and people have professed it since. As for myself, I did not find it so, nor, plainly, do I think a frog-pond, or a Walden Pond, contains the image of the ocean, even though there be water in both of them.

Both images, indeed, went back through all the steps, the degrees, the shadings of my education; and what we had been taught we should believe. "Love is enough, though the whole world be waning"—it may have been, and yet I doubt it: as for myself, I did not find it so.

And fame? She was another woman (of all love's rivals as I was to find, by a strange paradox, the only one by woman and by love beloved)—and all her shifting images, and all the guises of her loveliness, phantasmal, ghost-wise, like something flitting in a wood, I had dreamed of since my early youth—until her image and the image of the loved one had a thousand times been merged together. Now, I had her, as she may be had—and it was not enough.

These relics of the past were there. But life's weather had soaked in, and yet, I was not conscious yet what seepings had begun, or where, in what directions, the channel of my life was flowing. I was exhausted from my labor, respiring from the race, conscious only as is an exhausted runner that the race was over, the tape breasted, that he had won. This was the only thought within me at the time: the knowledge that I had met the ordeal a second time, and finally had conquered—conquered my desperation and my own self-doubt, the [51] fear that I could never come again to a whole and final accomplishment.

The circle goes full swing. The cycle draws to its full close. For four months, emptied, hollow, worn out, my life marked time, while my exhausted spirit drew its breath. And then the world came in again, upon the flood-tide of reviving energy. The world came in, the world kept coming in, and there was something in the world, and in my heart, I had not known of before.

I had gone back for rest, for recreation, for oblivion to that land which, of all the foreign lands that I had known, I loved best. I had gone back to it in hours of desperate confinement, of brain-fagged searching, in retrospect, in imagination, and in longing a thousand times from the giant jungle web of Brooklyn. I had gone back to it a thousand times, as men in prison pent, haltered to all the dusty shackles of the hour, the confused traffics of clamorous days, the wearying grayness of inevitable now, have longed for Cockaigne, for the haunted woods, the enchanted meadows, and the faery flood, the cloven rock. I had gone back to it in ten thousand dreams and memories of time and of desire—the sunken bell, the Gothic town, the plash of waters in the midnight fountain, the Old Place, the broken chime, and the blond flesh of secret, lavish women. I had gone back so in my memory and in desire a thousand times to Germany: and now that spring I was really there again—and no man ever had a happier or more fortuitous return.

Byron, they say, awoke one morning at the age of twenty-four, and found himself a famous man. Well, I had to wait some ten years longer, but the day came when I walked at morning through the Brandenburger Gate, and into the enchanted avenues of the faery green Tiergarten, and found that fame—or so it seemed to me—had come to me. For two months or more I had been away from home, had seen [52] no papers and had read no letters, had sought to find some easement, some slow and merciful release of the great coiled spring that was my mind and heart and very life that had been stretched to breaking point for years. And I had found it now in a series of oblivious wanderings that had led from Paris to Kent and from the Romney marshes up to London, and from London to the flat fecundity of Norfolk, and from Norfolk to the small and tidy smugness of the Dutch, and from Holland, as the train bore on, across the great and fertile tillage of Westphalia, to Hannover, old time-haunted town, and there across the kiefern-haunted forest of the North to vast Berlin. And now May had come again, and I walked below the mighty blossoms of the great horse chestnut trees, and through the Brandenburger Gate, and through the arcades of enchanted green, and felt, like Tamerlane, that it was passing great to be a king, and ride in triumph through Persepolis—and be a famous man.

After those long and weary years of Brooklyn and brute labor—of desperation and the need for proof to give some easement to my tormented soul—it was the easement I had dreamed of, the impossible faery, so impossibly desired, and now brought magically to life. It was—it seemed to be— the triumph and the glorious vindication of all that I had thought my life could be, that man could work for, or art achieve. The news of my success at home had come to Germany—where already I had been known for three years, and had achieved celebrity—and now, it seemed to me who had so often gone a stranger and unknown to the great cities of the world that now the whole of it was mine. The great town, the whole world was my oyster. Letters were there for me, and invitations: it seemed they had been waiting for me—and for three weeks there was a round of pleasure, celebration, [53] the wonderful thrill of meeting in a foreign land and in a foreign tongue a hundred friends, now for the first time known and captured—and May, and the cool nights, the glorious freshness of the air, the awakening of spring, the enchanted brevity of northern darkness, and glorious wine in slender bottles, and morning, and green fields, and pretty women—all of it was mine now, it seemed to have been created for me, to have waited for me, to exist and live in all its loveliness for my possession.

Three weeks passed so. By day there was the shining and the sapphire air, the horse chestnut trees, the singing sparkle of exultant life that swept through me across the town, so that at noon among the great crowds thronging the Kurfurstendamm, I also was a part of the green faery of the great Tiergarten park, and thence unto all crystal sparkles of Berlin, until I seemed to share it all, and all of it to be in me, as but a single, shining and exultant drop of water reflects and shares, and is a part of the million, million scallop shells of dancing light, and every lapping wave, and every white sail on the surface of the Wawnsee.

And there would be the singing of the air by day, the unheard singing of the blood, and the great crowds thronging the Kurfurstendamm, the gay and crowded terraces of the great cafes, and something, half-heard, half-suspected, coming from afar, a few flung seeds of golden music upon the air, the sudden music of the tootling fifes, and suddenly, the solid, liquid smack of booted feet, and young brown faces shaded under steel goose-stepping by beneath the green arcades of the Kurfurstendamm, the army lorries rolling past, each crowded with its regimented rows of young, formal, helmeted, armfolded and ramrodded bodies, and laughter, laughter in the crowd, and laughter rippling like a wave across the terraces of great cafes, [54] and bubbling like wine sparkles from the lips of all the pretty women—and all the singing and the gold of it was mine.

But something happened—I was not prepared. Too much gray weather had soaked through into my soul, and I could not forget. The memory of unrecorded days, the renaissance of brutal weathers, the excavation of the jungle trails—it all came back to me again insensibly, soaked through the shining brightness of that air, came through the latches of those clacking tongues, forced through at last its grim imponderable into the contours of those shining surfaces, the sense of buried meanings which not even May and magic and the Kurfurstendamm could help.

Sometimes it came to me with the desperate pleading of an eye, and the naked terror of a sudden look, the swift concealment of a sudden fear. Sometimes it just came and went as light comes, just soaked in, just soaked in—words, speech and action, and finally in the mid-watches of the night, behind thick walls and bolted doors and shuttered windows, the confession of unutterable despair, the corruption of man's living faith, the inferno of his buried anguish —the spiritual disease and death and strangulation of a noble and a mighty people.

And then day would come again, the cool glow of morning red, the bronze gold magic of the kiefern trees, the still green pools of lucid water, the faery stillness of the park and gardens of the great Tiergarten street—but none of it was the same as it had been before. For I had become aware of something else in life, as new as morning, and as old as Hell, and now articulated for the first time in a word, regimed now in a scheme of phrases and a system of abominable works. And day by day the thing soaked in, soaked in until everywhere, in every life I met, and in every life I touched, I met and saw and knew the ruin of its unutterable pollutions; and it still came [55] in, it kept coming in, so known now and understood at last beyond all depths of intellectual understanding, since the cancer and the root both came out of the body I had loved.

And now, another layer had been peeled off the gauzes of the seeing eye; and something had come into life that I had never seen before, but that now once seen and understood, I could never forget or be blind to again.

When I went back to America—to New York—the Fourth of July, my new-won fame was waiting at the boat, and, more faithful than with most, she abode with me through the winter of the furious season—but something cold and clear had come into my vision, and she no longer looked the same. Here, too, with this new mistress, I learned to see anew the world, and, seeing what fame was—such fame as I had won—and how desolately different from the goddess I had fancied her to be, I was not blinded. I saw that I had thought since childhood that she was the goal of my intent, and I saw I was mistaken. And with that further loss, I gained, as with all losses now, new hope: from every desperation came a fresh beginning, from every province of my exile, a new land. And I think I should be very grateful to her, for through her now the world that we have made, the structure of this life as we have fashioned it to be, came to me in a series of merciless revelations: and all the falseness of its false pretense, the easy barter of its given love—so lightly won by the moment's notoriety, so quickly vanished by the moment's loss—together with the huge conspiracy of the parasite—the whore, the harpy, the thief, the lawyer, the ambitious and the fashionable fool, the blackmailer, the contriving parasite—all rushing in like body lice, to suck and batten on the blood that fame has fattened. The ordeal began—two years and more of it —and through [56] it all in law, in court, in finance, in business, and society I came to know the corrupt and shoddy counterfeits of man. And, curiously, I was not disheartened. Curiously, I was not embittered, because for the first time in my life I was seeing clear and whole; and through the very failure of the thing I had so wanted to achieve, I was finding out at last the structure of things as they are. From this grim loss, and from the desolation of these new discoveries, I had derived, by a strange paradox, a new sense of life, a newer and, it seems to me, a better hope. For at the bottom of the well, at the rock bottom of the soil, in the whole corrupt and shoddy structure of the upper honeycomb, I had begun to see and understand and feel the common heart of man, and finally, I had come to see that this, no matter how much it gets betrayed, is the thing that can never be betrayed; no matter how much it gets corrupted, is the thing that finally can never be corrupted; no matter how much it gets defeated, is the thing that can never be defeated—the thing that is rock bottom at the end—the thing that will remain, that changes and is yet unchangeable—that endures and must endure.

The people! Yes, the people![19] The people that cannot ever be defeated or betrayed—the betrayed and the defeated people, the corrupted and the misguided people, the duped and superstitious people, the inert and the submissive people—but in the end, always the people!—just the people! —the rock bottom of the invincible and the everlasting people!

The rich people, yes!—The society people, yes!—The fashionable people, yes!—The fame-hunting and celebrity-chasing people, yes!—The pretty, reputation-loving, and bed-sleeping women, yes!—The publishers with their folk-lore and their mythology of benevolent and art-loving paternalism, yes!—The politicians and the rabble-rousers [57] and the far-seeing statesmen, yes!—The people gathered together at cocktail parties, talking about the latest plays, the latest books, the latest ideas, the latest talk, all in the most approved fashion, yes!—The college professors and instructors all talking their own varieties of the latest and most approved talk, yes!—All that they have come to be, all that the moment's fashion, or that the moment's need has made of them, all that they said, or thought that they thought, or felt that they felt, or believe that they believe—the whole systems of patterns that the structure of life which they have created and in which they have existed, have made of all of them!—I had seen and known them all now, in the cycle of my thirty-seven years—the dupe, the jester and the cheat; the snob, the parasite, the adept and the whore—all phases in the swing of the great cycle, all parts of it and the fame of things, and victims of it, and not to be hated or despised!—But at the end and

---

19 Perhaps it should be noted that Carl Sandburg's *The People, Yes* had been published and widely reviewed just two years before this was dictated.

always now, the eternal tide that changes always and that always is the same.

The people—yes, the people!—in the end, nothing but the people—on street corners and on the street, in subways and in crowded trains, in little towns and in great cities, at churches and at carnivals, upon the Eastern coast, and all across the continent—moving by day beneath immense and timeless skies, thronging the streets, the buildings, and the factories, the houses and the farms by day and all the million patterns of their daily schedules—but in the end, the only thing there is, the thing that lasts forever, and that cannot be betrayed—the people!

I had been long from home, and then one day I was home again.[20] [58] Eight years had passed, through the whole cycle of escape and flight, of exile and of desperate longing, of work, of failure, of accomplishment—I had lived my exile out in three thousand days and nights of exile and of desperate longing—of wanting to return until the very thought of it became an ache, the very fact of it a dream, a dream so intolerably vivid and intense that almost I could not believe it had ever been more solid substance than a dream. Oh, I had rebuilt it in my brain a million times—rebuilt it street by street, and house by house, and leaf by leaf, and stone by stone, until the very memory of all the faces burned there in my vision like the immortal memory of ghostly visitants from an unforgotten never-to-be-captured world—until I would awake and say—"There once was I—there once was such a boy as I—there once were certain people—such and such a town—there once this living flesh touched certain substances—there once this shoulder leaned against a certain tree—this foot was raised upon a certain step—there once this hand was grasped

20 Some of the ideas and phrases in this passage Wolfe had used before in his article entitled "Return," written for the Asheville *Citizen-Times,* May 16, 1937. In what he says here about the Parson and the brown-shirted thugs on his police force, Wolfe borrows heavily from one section of an article he had just published, "A Prologue to America," *Vogue,* February 1, 1938; see p. 151. The Parson is the name that Wolfe used for the political boss of Libya Hill (Asheville) in *You Can't Go Home Again.*

upon a certain rail—was clenched around a certain handle until almost I can feel the size and contour of its shape within my palm again—it must have been, it must have been—and yet—?"

I would rebuild it so there in my brain a million times with all the vividness of exile and of intolerable longing, to return and think—"It must have been—it must have been—and yet, perhaps I dreamed it. So many sundering floods have passed between—so many cities, countries, foreign lands, strange tongues and faces—so many, many jungle depths of time in Brooklyn, of work, of desperation, of love, of death, renewal, and fatigue—so many million, million things have come and gone, begun and ended, whole tides of this swarming and imperial world have passed between, the surge of oceans, and the [59] thrust of crowds, the forgotten memory of so many million, million men and words and facts and hours and places—it must be, yet it cannot—I have dreamed it: I'll go home again!"

Thinking—"I have a thing to tell them now—I'll go back again! I shall explain my reasons, and lay bare my purposes—reveal my life unto its heart's core, so nakedly that no man can doubt me! I'll go back some day and they shall hear me—we shall know each other utterly—they must understand! And I'll go back."

And seven years had passed, and I was long from home, and one day I went home again.

Ah well, well—dear friend, for here at this final hour, I turn to you in parting and farewell—you can't go home again: the tale is told now, the circle had full swing.

Hearing again the accents of remembered yesterdays, seeing again the fragments of the ruined town. "We're glad to see you—so you've come back again. We've missed you, now you ought to stay. Have you seen Bob yet? Jim's been looking for you. A lot of people ask about you. I know your family's glad to have you back. Sure; there was a lot of talk at first—a lot of them were pretty mad about the book—I guess you heard about it—but Hell! that's all over now! It's all forgotten; the only ones that are mad today

are those who think you should have put *them* in. Here's
Ed now: we're glad to see you. We've got the greatest place
on earth—so come on back to stay!"

The ruined town! The new and splendid buildings,
emptied even of the personnel they were to house—and
shining tunnels, glittering with tile, that leap through
mountains twixt the town and country where boys used to
swim—the monuments of brief grandeur, "fragments to
shore these ruins"—the blazing slope of concrete where the
green hill was—and new stamped-out hotels, and arcades,
shops and filling stations—the shining fragments of the
ruined town! At night, the Parson [60] smiles through his
artificial teeth and strokes his lantern jaws reflectively as
he looks out upon his ruined town. The hills are lovely,
even in the darkness, in the month of May—there has never
been a better year than this for dogwood, so the old men
say. The Parson smiles and strokes his lantern jaws reflectively, as he looks out on his ruined town. Even the hills
are lovely in the night—for on the hills, in mounting link-
ages, is sown light—and the splendid buildings, the million-dollar courthouse, the two-million-dollar city hall,
bathed silently in secret, lighted night, just like the nation's
Capitol at Washington, are modern, new, and, although
unpaid for, imposing to a stranger. All impresses by its
smartness now—even Parson's new police force, who are
young men now, spruce, lean, well-kept young men, so
different from their paunchy elders, so courteous to strangers when they park in the wrong place—such upstanding,
spruce, clean-cut young men: Americans, of course, of the
well-known Anglo-Saxon stock, and twenty-five years old,
and with natty, neat, new uniforms of brown—brown well-
pressed trousers and brown shoes, brown jaunty caps,
brown neckties, crisp brown shirts, brown cartridge belts
around the waist, and a whole arsenal of brown cartridges,
a brown holster, and the brown butt-end of a most busi-
ness-like six-shooter, hanging most formidably halfway
down the brown thigh, and strapped around the brown
leg with a brown thong—and with it all, such nice young
men, so courteous, so attentive and well-spoken to strangers

when they make mistakes—with something in their eyes,
however. Here is one I used to know; we went to school
when we were ten years old together, and we often shared
our lunch, and he was pitcher, I was first base on the
baseball team—and behind the smiles of greeting, something strange now, something changed through [61] rigid
pleatings of the mouth, the visage of the old lost boy looks
forth again—and there is something in his eyes, something
dead and hard and cold and furtive, in the eyes of all these
men in brown, that boys in school twenty years ago did
not have. The cops have shining motors now—and often,
in the quiet streets, in the still hours of the night, one will
find them, two together, silent, hard-eyed, hurrying, waiting. The saxophones are moaning low out at the Country
Club: the crowd is drunk, you can get good Scotch now,
although some of them still stick to corn. Two country kids
from Zebulon are sitting on the edges of their cells there
in the splendid million-dollar county jail: they are coming
round now, spitting through their bloody lips the fragments of their broken teeth and wondering just what
happened, for young cops in brown can be emphatic when
it comes to corn and kids from Zebulon; and in another
cell, another disturber of the peace and menace to the
public welfare is also spitting through his shredded teeth,
more casually, less reflectively—for he knows by now what
it is all about, and what he may expect from clean, upstanding brown-shirted cops who come upon a union or-
ganizer. Six hundred men, beneath the sweet young sod
of May, are rotting in their graves tonight, and sixty-eight
have shattered bullet fractures in their skulls; all still below,
and nothing stirs, except the turnings of the mute, compulsive worm; and up above, along the cool, leafed streets,
all silent, too, ten thousand other men are lying in their
beds, and not as dead men lie, but with gaunt sockets open,
and the eyes a-stare in darkness, ten thousand ruined men
above the earth are lying in their graves as well. Upon the
dead controls of the dead town rests the dead, corrupting
tyranny of the Parson's dead, compulsive hand—and the
Parson smiles through artificial teeth upon his crisp and

young brown-shirted force of clean young men tonight, and rubs reflectively his lantern jaws. [62]

And I? "There was a boy—ye know him well, you hills—" I had been long from home, and now I had come back again—and what is there to say?

Time passes and puts halters to debate. There was so much to say that could be spoken, there was so much to say that never could be said—there was so much to utter, that all unuttered, in my longing I had heard it, all un-spoken, spoken in mute passages of three thousand days and nights of exile and impossible desire—and now, I had come home again, and what is there to say?

Feeling the foot again upon the stair, the creak of the old tread, the sagging give of the old rail, feeling mute shapes in darkness pass about me, the rustling of a leaf, the huge imponderable still [*hiatus*] of the night, the cool of huge-starred mountain night again, and [*hiatus*] the awakened and unliving presences of yesterday—thinking— "I [*hiatus*] home again, here is the darkness, here the rail, here is the fo [*hiatus*] the tread—'there was a boy—ye knew him well, you hills'—I [*hiatus*] here, this was I—"

Seeking to find him in the remembered street, looki [*hiatus*] him by the ancient tree, trying to find him in the old house—[*hiatus*] wind stirs, and darkness moves about us, and there is the stil [*hiatus*] huge imponderable of night—"I was a boy here—where are the [*hiatus*] I was a boy here, this is I—"

You can't go home again.

To you, dear friend and parent of my spirit in my ye [*hiatus*] of search, I say farewell. The circle ends full swing: this [*hiatus*] of every man—a phrase in the great lexicon of what all li [*hiatus*] the cycle now is ended, and I say fare-well. I was the boy [*hiatus*] foot upon the stair, I was the child who had his shoul [*hiatus*] I was the youth of obscure parents who went out to [*hiatus*] [63] of this [*hiatus*] is Ameri [*hiatus*] knew the pride of youth, the sufferi [*hiatus*], the vanity, the egotism of youth, who knew its aspirat [*hiatus*] its high endeavor; I was the youth who went the road and traveled the long route through arrogance and scorn, the preciosities of lifeless and life-hating aesthetics; I was the youth who spoke the phrases, who learned the language, and who tried to shore up the feeling of his own wounded loneliness, insufficiency and self-doubt with the protective words of arrogance and scorn; I was the young man who learned to work, and in his work found first accomplishment; I was the lover, the love-stricken, love's tragedian in the little universe of love, love's martyr, love's forlorn; I was the exile, and the desperate explorer, the son you fathered in his time of need, the one you shielded from his own self-doubt, the one you aided nobly and with generous unselfishness to the accomplishment of his own fulfillment; I was the man, for thr [*hiatus*] years past, who founded on his own rock now, and now reliant on his own strength, knows now that henceforth he must find it only in himself because, like every man, he knows what he knows, he is what he is, he has what he has. And I know now that you can't go home again.

Therefore, dear friend, the time has come when each must go his way—you to that life you know the best, and to which now the years, the peril of the time, the loyalties of your own affiliation, and your conscience have now fixed and destined you forever—and to the past, and standing there upon its known and familiar shores; and I to mine— upon another shore, and facing after all these lives and deaths and births of things, a new land, and another hope.

TEXTUAL NOTES ON READING TEXT

Page:Line	Reading Text	Original Typescript
25:6	don't [in Mrs. Campbell's hand]	do not
26:1	has	is
26:16	last	this
27:3	blocks of granite	box of granites
27:4	smile, but	smile forgivingly, but
27:16	plain, bitter [ed.]	plain bitter
27:24	tempted [ed.]	attempted
27:27-28	writer too!	writer!
27:36	enroll.	enroll for his course.
28:5	*Post*, [ed.]	Post;
28:9	quite	decidedly
28:12	else [ed.]	else,
28:19	swift	script
28:19	action; [ed.]	action—
28:23	was an established [ed.]	was established
28:30	of	for
28:34	*Collier's*	Collier
29:32	*Post*,	Post
30:9	gentleman [ed.]	gentlemen
30:10	of "publics,"	of "markets," "publics,"
30:21	total	exceed
31:1	*yes*	yes
31:4	appeal	proposal
31:8	did	do
31:35	sense.	sense
31:36	mean [ed.]	mean,
31:39	writer,	writer
32:18	[From this point to page 44, line 39, the reader can collate the Reading Text with Wolfe's revised typescript by referring to Appendix I.]	
45:26	youth: [ed.]	youth;
45:30	desperate	definite
45:31	bodily, [ed.]	bodily;
45:34	suppose [ed.]	suppose,
46:9	better; [ed.]	better,
47:2	London	England
47:13	publisher,	publisher
47:15	time. When [ed.]	time—when
47:16-17	accepted. For [ed.]	accepted, for
48:20	it, expended	it; expended
48:23	period when I	period I
48:25	like, [ed.]	like;
49:3	finally, [ed.]	finally

Page:Line	Reading Text	Original Typescript
49:11	1929 [ed.]	1929,
49:27-28	been so hard on "the [Mrs. Campbell's long-hand correction]	been "the
49:29	1923 —	1923,
49:33	world	life
49:34	1929,	1929
50:17	this	*this*
50:22	from	in
50:37	him. In [ed.]	him—in
51:23	press; in	press; and in
51:25	and all	and in all
51:33	town [ed.]	town;
52:18	that	but
52:28	that for [ed.]	before
52:31	but a delusion	but delusion
53:3	old, [ed.]	old
53:4	again, [ed.]	again;
53:5	work, [ed.]	work;
53:10	world, indeed,	world indeed
53:13	grow, [ed.]	grow
54:5	society, [ed.]	society—
54:11	differently,	differently
54:17	still so absorbed	still absorbed
54:24	involved, [ed.]	involved;
55:15	salaries. I [ed.]	salaries; I
55:16	friends. Two [ed.]	friends—two
55:21	radio, [ed.]	radio;
55:22	market, [ed.]	market
55:24	fortune. I [ed.]	fortune; I
55:28	it; [ed.]	it,
55:36	seated; [ed.]	seated—
55:38	Tony must be	Tony would be
56:10	distinguished-looking [ed.]	distinguished looking
56:12-13	jolly-looking [ed.]	jolly looking
56:14	Kahn's	Kahn
56:15	balloon; [ed.]	balloon,
56:23-24	there before the fire.	there.
56:27-28	And looking back,	And, looking back
57:9	time: [ed.]	time;
57:27	worked. I [ed.]	worked—I
58:9	men, both young and old, [ed.]	men both young and old
58:23	flowers seemed [ed.]	flowers had seemed
58:25	incredible; [ed.]	incredible,
58:30	help; [ed.]	help,
58:31	great, [ed.]	great
58:34	were on their [ed.]	was on its
58:35	occasionally I saw Scott	occasionally Scott
58:39	passed. Late [ed.]	passed: late

Page:Line	Reading Text	Original Typescript
59:3	is	was
59:5	cool, [ed.]	cool
59:6	Forest; [ed.]	Forest,
59:9	dry, hard, [ed.]	dry hard
59:9	wooden sound	sound
59:12	manure. I [ed.]	manure; I
59:12	excited, [ed.]	excited
59:26	much, [ed.]	much
59:27	They [Mrs. Campbell's long-hand correction]	There
59:30	America? [ed.]	America, —
59:31	prosperity, of high wages, [ed.]	prosperity—of high wages—
59:36	happen? [ed.]	happen?—
60:4-5	bitter want at	bitter at
60:7	dumb	dung
60:11	knew, [ed.]	knew
60:16	down, [ed.]	down
60:22	restraint, [ed.]	restraint—
62:10	do? [ed.]	do.
62:27	means,	means
62:31	effrontery, and [ed.]	effrontery and,
62:32	dishonesty, [ed.]	dishonesty
62:32	conversions [ed.]	conversions,
64:21	discovering, [ed.]	discovering
65:5	life	life,
65:5	work	work,
65:9	this: [ed.]	this: —
65:13	write again	write, again
65:34	my	the
65:38	head. [ed.]	head
66:1	[From this point to page 70, line 37, the reader can collate the Reading Text with Wolfe's revised typescript by referring to Appendix I.]	
70:38-39	the Fourth of July [,]	in the autumn of that year—
70:39	and,	and
71:1	than with most	than most
71:11-12	every province of my exile	every exiled province
71:15	be, [ed.]	be
71:18	loss—[ed.]	loss:
71:27	embittered, [ed.]	embittered;
71:33	and, it	and, as it
71:37	the	a
72:1	corrupted, is	corrupted, it is
72:2	defeated, is	defeated, it is
72:5	is yet	is as yet
72:6	endure. [ed.]	endure—
72:7	The people! Yes [ed.]	—The people! Yes
72:13	people! [ed.]	people!—
72:26	all that the moment's	all of the moment's

Page:Line	Reading Text	Original Typescript
72:27	need has made	need have made
73:2	always is the same[.]	never changes—
73:3	The people—yes [ed.]	—The people—yes
73:12	people! [ed.]	people! —
73:22	dream. [ed.]	dream —
73:26-27	never-to-be-captured [ed.]	never to be captured
74:4	yet — ?" [ed.]	yet?"—
74:6	longing,	longing
74:8	it. So [ed.]	it — So
74:13-14	ended, whole	ended, the whole
74:18	yet it cannot —	yet — cannot —
74:18	again!" [ed.]	again! —"
74:20	again! [ed.]	again! —
74:22	me! [ed.]	me! —
74:24	understand! [ed.]	understand! —
74:24	back." [ed.]	back —"
74:26	again. [ed.]	again —
74:29	swing. [ed.]	swing —
74:30	Hearing [ed.]	— Hearing
74:32	again. [ed.]	again —
74:33	stay. [ed.]	stay —
74:33	yet? [ed.]	yet? —
74:34	you. [ed.]	you —
74:34	you. I [ed.]	you — I
74:35	back. [ed.]	back —
74:39	now! [ed.]	now! —
75:1	*them*	them
75:1	in. [ed.]	in —
75:2	you. We've [ed.]	you — we've
75:4	The ruined [ed.]	— The ruined
75:10	stamped-out [ed.]	stamped out
75:12	town! [ed.]	town! —
75:20	is [ed.]	are
75:20-21	million-dollar [ed.]	million dollar
75:21	two-million-dollar [ed.]	two million dollar
75:23	Washington, [ed.]	Washington —
75:23	and,	and
75:24	stranger. All [ed.]	stranger — all
75:32	brown jaunty [ed.]	brown, jaunty
76:2	however. Here [ed.]	however — here
76:2	know;	know,
76:13-14	waiting. [ed.]	waiting —
76:16	corn. Two [ed.]	corn — two
76:18	million-dollar [ed.]	million dollar
76:25	casually, [ed.]	casually
76:28	organizer. [ed.]	organizer —
76:33	too, [ed.]	too, —
76:35	a-stare	astare
76:36	well. [ed.]	well —

Page:Line	Reading Text	Original Typescript
76:37	town [ed.]	town,
76:37	rests	the rest
76:39	crisp [ed.]	crisp,
77:2	jaws. [ed.]	jaws —
77:3	And I?	And we?
78:10-11	the son	a son
78:11	time of need	time of desperate effort and of need

APPENDIX I

PASSAGES OF THE DICTATED SPEECH REVISED FOR USE IN "YOU CAN'T GO HOME AGAIN"

In the following pages one can see Wolfe at work revising passages of the dictated Purdue Speech for use in the novel that was to be entitled *You Can't Go Home Again*. Seven of the revised pages—18 through 24—were so nearly what he wanted at the moment that instead of copying them out longhand he merely pre-empted them as sheets of manuscript for the novel. In the Thomas Wolfe Collection of William B. Wisdom in the Houghton Library at Harvard University, where the manuscript of the novel is located, there is a carbon copy of a typescript of it that incorporates a few minor changes. Whether this transcript was made before or after Wolfe's death is uncertain. In any event, drastic changes were made before the novel was published.

Wolfe had expected to do a great deal more work on the manuscript before submitting it to the printer. Since his unexpected death prevented this, the task fell to his editor, Edward Aswell. *The Web and the Rock* appeared in 1939, the year after Wolfe's death, and *You Can't Go Home Again* the next year, with no indication of the major role Aswell had played in preparing these novels for publication. But in the third book to come from the enormous stack of manuscript left by Wolfe, *The Hills Beyond*, Aswell included a revealing essay. In "A Note on Thomas Wolfe" he says that "the wonderful thing" about Wolfe's manuscript was that "once the extraneous matter was removed, once the unfinished fragments and great chunks of stuff that did not belong in the book were taken out, the parts that remained fell into place and fitted together like the pieces of a jigsaw puzzle."

Something of Aswell's editorial method is revealed in
what happened to revised sections of the Purdue Speech
before they got into the novel. In three of the revisions
Wolfe introduced the name of Dexter Joyner, yet none of
these references appear in the published narrative. In response to inquiries about this character, Richard S. Kennedy wrote in a letter to the editors that notes by Wolfe
clearly indicate his intention of having Dexter Joyner in
the novel as a fully developed character, an aesthete, who
was to appear first in Libya Hill during George Webber's
boyhood, to reappear at George's college, and then to turn
up again in New York; but that since Wolfe never developed him fully enough, as he did Nebraska Crane and
Jerry Alsop, Aswell cut him out of the narrative.

Through this character Wolfe had intended to ridicule
passing fads among aesthetes of the twenties and the thir-
ties. A manuscript outline quoted by Kennedy (Harvard
College Library, 46 AM—[24-S]) indicates that Wolfe at
one time thought of following Dexter Joyner through
changes of opinion and attitude:

Joyner

1923:	The Waste Land
	Harlem
	Charles Chaplin as Hamlet
	Joyner's Novel: The Venetian Countess Comes to Harlem
	The Fourteen Modern Arts
1925:	Joyner now in Paris: "The Revolution of the Word"—Dada
1926:	The Sun Also Rises on Mr. Joyner
1929:	The Crash: Joyner's Return Home—Humanism
1930-1931:	Joyner: The Coming of the Revolution
1931-1935:	The Revolution Triumphant
1935:	The Revolution on the Wane—Mr. Trotsky

Kennedy adds: "You will note that this is a really conglom-
erate character, which Wolfe developed out of his associa-

tion with Kenneth Raisbeck," the original of the aesthete Starwick in *Of Time and the River;* Gilbert Seldes, author of *The Seven Lively Arts;* Elinor Wylie, author of *The Venetian Glass Nephew;* Carl Van Vechten, author of *The Tattooed Countess* and *Nigger Heaven;* Edwin Berry Burgum and V. F. Calverton, both Marxist literary critics; "and I would also add Lincoln Kierstein," editor of *Hound and Horn,* "and probably others who reflected some of the literary enthusiasms indicated above."

Although excluded from the narrative about George Webber, Dexter Joyner did get into print. The year after Wolfe's death his *A Note on Experts: Dexter Vespasian Joyner* was published by the House of Books, Ltd., New York, in an edition limited to 300 copies. No editor is named, but the booklet, only twenty pages long, was copyrighted by Maxwell Perkins, executor of the Wolfe estate. It presents two portraits etched in vitriol. Without naming the reporter or his newspaper, the first sketch portrays the New York *Herald Tribune* reporter who looked at some of Wolfe's personal papers while Wolfe was out getting a drink for him, and then garbled and distorted the interview, all for the purpose of "getting a good story." But, Wolfe says, you know where you stand with "this kind of whore." Then he presents "a worse type"—Dexter Vespasian Joyner—"the greatest expert I ever knew." Noting Dexter's "flexible adaptability," his "chameleon-like change," he tells what a snob Dexter was when he came to college in the South after a year at Yale. Dexter referred to Wolfe and his friends as "yockels" (yokels). After they formed a "Yockels Club," Dexter left, "yockeled out of college." He went to Harvard, and then to Oxford. The account of him ends there, with an anecdote telling how on one occasion, after a snobbish remark, he is effectively silenced by a don.

Besides omitting the references to Dexter Joyner, Aswell made other changes, some of them stylistic. By referring to the pages of *You Can't Go Home Again* cited in the margin, one can see how passages of the speech were ultimately adapted for the novel. The closing chapters of Kennedy's

The Window of Memory: The Literary Career of Thomas Wolfe contain enlightening discussion of Aswell's "creative editing."

Explanation of Symbols Used

Italics indicate canceled words, lined through by pencil.

Pointed brackets, < >, enclose additions in longhand, by Wolfe unless otherwise indicated.

Square brackets, [ ], enclose editorial matter.

The bracketed figure [§] indicates the end of a leaf of the original typescript of the dictated speech.

For checking passages in *You Can't Go Home Again* referred to in the margin, either Harper's trade edition or the Harper's Modern Classics edition may be used; the pagination of the two is the same.

[*In the left margin* <♯ [/] Begin [/]——— [/] In book>]

Twenty years ago, when I was seventeen years old, and a *student* <sophomore> at *Chapel Hill* <old Pine Rock>—*which is the University in the my native state of North Carolina*—I was very fond, along with many of my fellows, of talking about my "philosophy of life." We were very earnest about it. It seems to me that we were always asking one [*hiatus*] our philosophy of life. I'm not sure now what [*hiatus*] time, *except that* <but> I am sure [*A large crossmark was penciled through the preceding lines, presumably after Wolfe had made use of them in revised form.*] [§] I had one. <Everybody had.> We were deep in philosophy at *Chapel Hill* <Pine Rock>—we juggled about such formidable terms as "concepts," "moments of negation," and so on, in a way that would have made Spinoza blush; and [*revised* blush. And] if I do say so, I was no slouch at it myself. It would surprise *many* <some> people today to know that at the age of seventeen I had an A-1 [*revised* a-1] rating as philosopher—"concepts," [*comma canceled*] *had* <held> no terrors *in* <for> my young life, *I could lead with a "concept" and counter with a* <and> "moment<s> of negation" *in a way that would even put Joe Louis to shame:* <were my meat.> I could split a hair with the best of them, and now that I have *gone in* <turned> definitely *for* <to> boasting, I made a one in Logic, and it was said it was the only

Bottom of Leaf 10

[*See YCGHA, p. 708.*]

Leaf 11

[*See YCGHA,*
p. 709.]

one that had been given in that course for twenty years. So *you see,* when it comes to speaking of philosophy, there is one before you who is privileged to speak.

I don't know how it goes with students of this day and generation *here in Indiana,* but I know that to *the* students twenty years ago at *Chapel Hill* <Pine Rock College>, "philosophy" was a most important thing. We stayed up nights and talked about it. We discussed the idea of God most earnestly: truth, goodness, beauty *was* <were> our meat—we [*revised* meat. We] had ideas about these things, and <,> believe me, I do not laugh at them today: we [*revised* today. We] were young, we were impassioned, and *it was not bad.* <we were sincere.> One of the more memorable events of my college career occurred one day at noon, when I was coming up a campus path and encountered coming toward me one of my colleagues *whom I shall call B. C.* <whose name was D. T> Jones—[*dash canceled*] *largely because that happens to be his name.* [§] *BC* <D. T.> Jones <—sometimes also known as Delirium Tremens Jones, for reasons that may presently appear—> was also a philosopher, and [*revised* philosopher. And] the moment I saw him coming towards me I knew that *B. C.* <D. T> Jones was in the throes. *B. C.* <D. T> was red-haired, gaunt and angular, he had red eyebrows and red eyelids—he had *come from* <been one of> a <large> family of primitive Baptists before he came to *Chapel Hill* <old Pine Rock>—and now as he came toward me, everything about him, hair, eyebrows, eyelids, eyes, freckles, and

Leaf 12

even the knuckles of his large and bony hands <,> were excessively and terrifically red. <¶> He was coming up from *Battle* <Joyner> Park, which was a noble wood, in which we held initiations and in which we took our Sunday strolls. It was also the place where we went alone when we were struggling with the problems of philosophy. It was where we went when we were going through what was known as "the wilderness experience," and it was the place from which triumphantly, when "the wilderness experience" was done, we emerged. *B. C.* <D. T.> was emerging now: he had been there, he told me <later, all night long,> for the past eighteen hours, his [*revised* hours. His] "wilderness experience" had been a good one—he came bounding toward me like a kangaroo, leaping into the air in intervals, and the first and only word<s> he said *was:* <were:> "I've had a Concept!" And then he passed—he left me stunned and fastened, [*comma canceled*] *plastered* to an ancient tree, as *B. C.* <D. T.> went on down the path, high-bounding, kangaroo-like, every step or two, to carry the great news to the host.

And yet I do not laugh at it. We were young men in those days, <but> we were earnest and impassioned ones, and each of us had his philosophy. And all of us—this was the sum and root of it—had his "Philosopher." He was a noble and a venerable man—one of those great figures that almost every college had some [§] twenty years ago; and that I hope they still have. For fifty years, he had been a dominant and leading figure in the life of the whole

[*See YCGHA, p. 710.*]

Leaf 13

state: in his teaching he was, I think, what is known as a Hegelian—I know the process of his scholastic reasoning was intricate —and *then* <came> up out of ancient Greece through a great series of "developments" to Hegel—and after [after *underlined by typewriter*] Hegel—he did not supply the answer, but after [after *underlined by typewriter*] Hegel was our <own> Old Man. <¶> Looking back, *all that* <our philosopher's "philosophy"> does not seem important now— [*dash canceled*] our philosophers "philosophy"—[*dash canceled, period added*] looking [*revised* Looking] back, it seems at best a tortuous and patched up scheme. But what was most important was the man himself: he was a great teacher, and what he did for us, what he had done for people in *that state* <Catawba> for fifty years, was not to give them his "philosophy"— but to communicate to them his own alertness, his originality, his power to think. <¶> To us, he was a vital force, because he supplied *the* <to> many of us, for the first time in our lives, the inspiration of a questioning intelligence. He *talk* <taught> us not to be afraid to think, to question; to examine critically the most venerable of our native superstitions, our local prejudices, to look hide-bound conventions in the eye and challenge them. In these ways, he was a powerful and moving figure—[*dash canceled, period added*] <Throughout the state,> the bigot hated him—[*dash canceled, semicolon added*] but his own students worshipped him to idolatry. And the seed he planted grew—the deposit of his teaching stayed—even when

Hegel, concepts, moments of negation, had all gone, or had merged back into the confused and tortuous pattern from which they were derived. [§]

<¶> About this time, I began to write. I was editor of the college paper—<The Old Pine Rock—a rock> which, in my day, and under my direction, always did have <,> at least, a certain *archaeological interest*—[*dash canceled*] <geological distinction> since it was interesting to examine in this week's edition the ruins and relics of last month's news. But in addition to this, I wrote some stories and some poems for *the* <our> magazine, [*comma canceled*] <—The Burr—> of which I was also a member of the editorial staff. <¶ Gerald Alsop was the editor that year, and my brilliant cousin, Dexter Joyner, had been editor a year or two before, —before he shook our common clay out of his shoes, and departed for more aesthetic climes.> The War was going on then; I was too young to be in service, and I suppose my first attempts creatively may be traced to the direct and patriotic inspiration of the War. I remember one, in particular—a poem, I believe, my first, which [*revised* poem, (I believe my first) which] was aimed directly at the luckless head of Kaiser Bill. The poem was called defiantly "The *Challenge* <Gauntlet>", and I remember it was written *directly* in the style, and according to the meter, of the present crisis [*revised* "The Present Crisis"], by James Russell Lowell. <¶> I remember further that it took a high tone from the very beginning: the poet, it is said, is the prophet and the bard—the

Leaf 14

[*See YCGHA, p. 711.*]

awakened tongue of all his folk—and I was all of that. In the name of embattled democracy, I let the Kaiser have the works, and I remember two lines in particular that seemed to me to have a very ringing tone—"Thou hast given us the challenge—pay, *now* <thou> dog, the cost, and go!" I remember these lines so well because they were the occasion of an editorial argument at the time: the more conservative element on the editorial staff, <led by Jerry Alsop,> felt that the words, "thou dog" <,> were too [§] strong—not that the Kaiser didn't deserve it, but that they jarred rudely upon the high moral elevation of the poem, and upon the literary quality of the *Carolinian magazine* <The Burr.> Above my own vigorous protest, they were deleted. <¶ And> I also remember writing another poem that year, which was the spring of 1918, <a cheerful one> about a peasant in a Flander's field who ploughed up a skull, and then went on quietly about his work, while the great guns blasted far away. [*period canceled, comma added*] <and "the grinning skull its grisly secret keeps."> I also remember a short story—my first—which was called "A *Cullenden* <Winchester> of Virginia" —which was about *a* <the> recreant son of an old family who recovers his courage, and vindicates his tarnished honor in the last charge over the top that takes his life. These, so far as I can recall them, were my first creative efforts; it will be seen what an important part the last War played in them.

I mention all this just to indicate what has happened to me in the last twenty

Leaf 15

years, and because of its reference also to a charge that has sometimes been made by some of my friends. *One of them* <Hunt Conroy>, for example, <who is> not more than three or four years my senior, is very fixed in his assertion of what he calls "the lost generation"—a generation of which <, as you know,> he has been quite vociferously a member, and in which he has tried enthusiastically to include me. <We used to argue about it all one Summer long *when I was at* in Switzerland when he was at Vevey, and I at Montreux.> "You belong to it, too," he used to say <grimly>. "You came along at the same time. You can't get away from it, you're [*revised* it. You're] a part of it whether you want to be or not"—to which my vulgar response *has been:* <would be> "Don't *you* you-hoo me!"

[*See YCGHA, p. 715.*]

If *my friend* <Hunt> wants [wants *underlined by typewriter*] to belong to the Lost Generation <—> and it really is astonishing with what fond eagerness *these* <some> people [§] hug the ghost of desolation to their breast—that's his affair. But he can't have me. If I have been elected, it has been against my <knowledge and my> will; and I *hereby* resign. I don't feel that I belong to a lost generation, and I have never felt so. Furthermore, I doubt very much the existence of a lost generation, except insofar as every generation, groping, must be lost. In fact, it has occurred to me recently, that if such a thing as a lost generation does exist in our own country, it is probably more those men of advanced middle age who spoke the

Leaf 16

language, and who know no other now, than the language that was spoken before 1929. These men indubitably are lost. But I am not one of them, and I don't think <I> was ever part of any lost generation anywhere. The fact remains, however, I was lost. And the fact that I no longer feel so is *the fact that* <what> I am going to *try to* describe *now*.

[See YCGHA, p. 716.]

It is *perhaps* a little premature to start summing up one's life experience at the age of thirty-seven, and I *shall* certainly do not intend to do so <here>. But, although thirty-seven is not a very great age to have learned many things, it is time enough to have learned a few. Rather, it seems to me, by that time a man has lived long enough to look back over his life and see certain events and periods in a proportion and a perspective he could not have had at the time when they occurred. I think that has happened to me, and since each of those periods really represent to me a pretty marked change and development not only in my whole view about *writing* <the work I do,> but in my views on men and living *and the work I do,* and my own [§] relation to the world *around me,* I am going to *try to describe them to you* <tell about them> now.

[See YCGHA, pp. 707-708.]

Leaf 17

For the sake of convenience, I am going to begin at the time when I was about twenty years old, *because I suppose that is about the age of many of you who are here tonight. Furthermore, it* <That> is a convenient date because it marks the *date* <time> of my graduation from <Pine Rock> college, and the time when I was just beginning to hint timidly to myself that I might one day try to be professionally a writer. At that time, I did not dare go further than suggest this ambition to myself in the most hesitant and tentative fashion, and that period of hesitancy and reserve was to continue for at least six years before I ever dared to commit myself boldly and wholeheartedly to the proposition that I was a writer, and that henceforth that [that *underlined by pencil*] should be the work I did. Therefore, that first cycle, from about 1920 to 1926, is the one I am going to tell you about first.

Looking back, in an effort to see myself as I was in those days, I am afraid I was not *always* a very friendly or agreeable *person* <young man>. The plain truth of the matter is that I was carrying a chip on my shoulder, and I suppose I was daring the whole world to knock it off. The chip on my shoulder had, of course, to do with writing, and with the life I wanted to lead. And I suppose the reason I was outwardly so truculent at times and inclined to be arrogant and take a high tone with people who, it seemed to me, doubted my ability to do the thing I wanted to do, was that inwardly I was by no means <so> arrogantly sure that I could do it myself. It was a form of whistling to keep one's courage up. [§]

[See YCGHA, p. 722.]

<Yet,> When [*revised* when] I *was graduated from college in 1920* <returned and was graduated from Pine Rock the following year—> I was *then really just nineteen* <only twenty then—> I don't suppose it would have been possible to

Leaf 18
[See YCGHA, p. 716.]

find a more confused or baffled person than I was. I had been sent to college *in order* to "prepare myself for life"—as the phrase went in those days—and it almost seemed that the total effect of my college training was to produce in me a state of utter unpreparedness. I had come from *what is, I think,* one of the most conservative parts of America, and from one of the most conservative elements of American life. So far as I know, all of my people until a generation before, had been country people, whose living had been in one way or another derived *from* <out of> the earth. Only within the past generation really had any of them <—the Joyners—> "moved into town," and become business <and professional> men—lumber dealers, contractors, <lawyers> and so forth. <¶> My father *himself* <, John Webber,> had been all his life a working man. He had done hard labor with his hands since the time he was twelve years old. <As *you know,* I have told you,> He [*revised* he] was a man of great natural ability and of a great deal of natural intelligence, and like many other men *of this class,* who have been deprived of the advantages of a formal education themselves, he was *too* ambitious for his son, and wanted him to have one. It is but natural that people of this kind should endow formal education with a kind of magic practicality: a college was a kind of magic door which opened to a man not only all the reserves of learning, but provided him with a kind of passport to success, a kind of magic key to the great material rewards of

[*See YCGHA, p. 717.*]

place or money that the world has to offer.
Further, it is but natural that a man like
this should seek for that success along one
of the roads that had always been approved, [*comma canceled; period added*]
and <¶> the [*revised* The] road that he
<had> chose<n> for me *was law. I think
he had himself cherished all his life an
ambition to study law, and I think he had
always regretted the accident of birth and
of necessity that had prevented him from
study*— <, before his death in 1916, was   *Verso of*
some branch of engineering. I know that   *Leaf 18*
he would [§] have stubbornly opposed the
Joyner choice—which, in devotion to *the
memory of* our obscure kinship with the
illustrious Zachariah—was the law. The
old man had small use for the law as a
profession, and, with the exception of his
friendship with Judge Robert Joyner, I
think he had very little respect for the
lawyer as a man:> [§] *ing it, and in a way*   *Leaf 19*
*I had been chosen as a kind of fulfillment
of his own ambition. By 1920, it was already apparent that whatever I would be,
I would never be a lawyer. By that time
my father was old and sick, and had only
a year or two more to live, and I knew that
I had grievously disappointed him. For*   [*See YCGHA,*
that reason alone, <For all these reasons,>   *p. 718.*]
it was difficult to admit, even to myself,
the stirrings of *a desire to write;*— <a desire so fantastic and impractical as the
desire to write. It only confirmed the
worst suspicions that my people had of me
—suspicions, I fear, that had begun to eat
into my own opinion of myself. Conse-
quently,> the first admission that I made

to myself was an evasive one. I told myself that I wanted to go into journalism,
and the first work that I looked for was
newspaper work. Looking back, the reason for this decision now seems transparently clear: I doubt very much that I had
at that time the burning enthusiasm for
newspaper work that I thought I had, but
I convinced myself that I did have it, because newspaper work provided me with
the only means I knew whereby I could, in
some fashion, write, and earn a living.
<¶> To have confessed openly to my
family at that time an outspoken desire to
be "a writer" would have been impossible.
And the reason why it would have been
impossible was that in their consciousness
—as well as in my own—"a writer" was a
very remote kind of person, a romantic
figure like Lord Byron, or Longfellow or
—or—Irvin S. Cobb—who in some magical
way was gifted with the power to write
poems and stories and novels that were
printed in books or in the pages of magazines like The Saturday Evening Post—and
who, for all these reasons, was a very
strange, mysterious kind of person, who
lived a very strange, mysterious and glittering sort of life, and who came from
some strange and mysterious and glittering sort of world, very far away from any
life or any world that we [we *underlined
by typewriter*] had ever known. <¶> That,
I believe, represents pretty accurately the
image we all had in our minds about "a
writer"—and I believe it represents pretty
accurately the image many people have today. I don't think *my own family,* <the

Joyners,> for example < (including the distinguished Dexter)>, have [§] ever quite recovered from their own astonishment that I was, or was said to be, "a writer"; and if I had openly announced my intention of being one at the age of twenty, they would have been decidedly alarmed. And the reason they would have been alarmed—and later on were alarmed, when I did announce it—was that the whole thing would have seemed so fantastic and improbable to them. To be a writer was, in modern phrase, "nice work if you could get it"—if you could be a writer like Lord Byron or Longfellow or Irvin S. Cobb—but *for one of the family,* for a boy who had grown up in the town of *Asheville* <Libya Hill>, *North Carolina* <Catawba>, in *Buncombe* <Holcombe> County—who had, it is true, sold [sold *underlined by typewriter*] The Saturday Evening Post on the streets of *Asheville* <Libya Hill> (if that [that *underlined by typewriter*] was any sort of training for a writer)—now to openly assert he was [was *underlined by typewriter*] one, or was going to be, bordered on the fringes of lunacy. It harkened back to the days of Uncle *Greeley* <Perdy Joyner>, who spent all his time learning to play the violin, and who borrowed fifty dollars from Uncle *Jim* <Burn> one time to take a course in phrenology. I had always been told that there was a strong resemblance in appearance between myself and Uncle *Greeley* <Perdy>, and now I knew if I confessed my secret desires, the resem-

Leaf 20

[*See YCGHA,
p. 719.*]

blance would seem to be a great deal more marked than ever.

Well, it [*revised* It] was a painful situation, <and> it was, in many ways, an amusing one—it [*revised* one. It] seems to me to be always such a human and American one, and it must be familiar to *you* <us> all. At any rate, it was to shape the course of my life for years. *That summer after graduation things turned out fortunately for me so that I got money whereby I could go to Harvard and enroll in the graduate school for a year. And after that year was over, I managed to get money to go there for two years more, so that I was there for three years in all. Looking back upon that experience, I can see it now in a* [§] [*One assumes that Wolfe intended the next two lines to be canceled like those immediately preceding and following*] clearer perspective. At the time, I don't think I knew clearly my reason for wanting to go to Harvard, except that I was still marking time, *and couldn't clearly decide what I did want to do. But I argued strongly for the Harvard move on the ground that it would give me the chance to do graduate work and to get a graduate degree, both of which, I argued, would be useful to me no matter what I later did. The real reason was that I wanted to write, and this move, groping as it was, was nevertheless some further effort toward it.* [*The rest of this paragraph has a large crossmark through it and a vertical line by it in the left margin.*] At Chapel Hill I had begun to write one act plays under the

Leaf 21

direction of Professor Frederick Koch, who had come there while I was a student and established the organization which has now become widely known as The Carolina Playmakers. Several of these plays had been produced there by the Playmakers with some success, and now, at Harvard, it was not only natural but almost inevitable that I should seek for admission in the late Professor George Pierce Baker's Forty-seven Workshop. Thus, it turned out almost immediately that my graduate work at Harvard developed mainly into the business of writing plays—although it is true I took some other courses and picked up a Master's degree more or less incidentally, on the way.

From this point begins a newer development. At Harvard, <My cousin, Dexter Joyner was already there, already one of the shining ornaments of a glittering coterie, and although his acknowledgment of my existence had heretofore not proceeded further than a supercilious nod, I found that a country cousin with six thousand dollars was not wholly without honor even on Eleventh street. At any rate in *the Bohemian precincts of* what I swiftly learned to call the village> for the first time in my life, I was thrown into the company of a group of sophisticated young people—at least, they seemed very sophisticated to me in those days. Instead of people like myself, who had felt within themselves the timid but unspoken flutterings of a desire to write, and to be a writer, here were people who openly asserted that they were.

[See YCGHA, p. 719.]

[*See YCGHA,*
p. 720.]
Leaf 22

They not only openly asserted that they were, but they openly asserted that a great many other people that I had thought were, [*comma canceled*] [§] most dismally were not. I began to discover that when I made some hesitant effort to take a part in the brilliant conversation that flashed around me, I must be prepared for some very rude shocks. For example, it was decidedly disconcerting to a *Chapel Hill* <Libya Hill and Pine Rock> youth of twenty *years* <one>, when he eagerly asked another *Harvard* youth of not much more than that: "Have you ever read Galsworthy's 'Strife'?"—to have that other youth raise his eyebrows slowly, and then say in an accent of resigned regret: "I *am* <'m> sorry. I can't read him. I simply can't read him. Sorry—" with a kind of rising inflection, as if to say it was too bad, but that the situation simply could not be helped. <¶> They were "sorry" about and for a great many other things *in* <and> people, <—> too — [*dash canceled, comma added*] too many, it now seems as I look back, for it seems that there was hardly a leading figure writing for the theatre in those days who escaped their censure [.] Shaw, for example, was "amusing"—but he was not a dramatist, he had never learned how to write a play, O'Neill's reputation was grossly exaggerated—his dialogue was clumsy, and his characters stock types; Barrie was insufferable on account of his sentimentality; as for Pinero, Jones, and others of that ilk, their productions were already so dated that they were laughable—in fact, almost everyone was out of step <,> one gathered <,> except our own particular small groups of Jims. And our own particular small group of Jims were by no means sure of one another—it [*revised* another. It] was usually a case of "everyone's wrong but thee and me, and even thee is for the most part wrong."

In a way, this superior criticality [*revised* super-criticality] was a very good thing [§] for me—it [*revised* me. It] taught me to be a good deal more critical and questioning about some of the most venerated names and reputations of the day, whose authority had been handed down to me by the preceptors of the past <,> and which I had accepted in too unquestioning a way. But the trouble with it was that I was now tied up in the speeches of niggling and over-refined aestheticism, which it seems to me, was not only pallid and precious <,> but too detached from life to provide the substance and the inspiration of high creative work. <¶> It is interesting to look back now and to see just what it was we did believe ten or fifteen years ago—these bright young men and women of the time, who wanted to produce something of value to the arts. We talked a great deal about "art and beauty"—a great deal about "the artist"; it now seems to me that on the whole the total deposit of this was bad. It was bad because it gave to young people who were deficient in the vital materials and experiences of life, and in the living contacts which the artist ought to have with life, the language and the for-

Leaf 23

[*See YCGHA, p. 721.*]

mulas of an unwholesome preciosity. <¶>
We talked about "the artist" a great deal
too much; looking back, it seems to me
that the creature we conceived in our
imagination as "the artist" was a kind of
aesthetic Frankenstein. Certainly, he was
not a living man. And <if> the artist,
[*comma canceled*] <is not> first and foremost a living man—and by this I mean a
man of life, a man who belongs to life, who
is connected with it, and who draws the
sources of his strength from it—then what
kind of man is he? <¶> The artist we
talked about *is* <was> not this kind of
man at all, indeed, if he had any existence
at all, except the existence that we gave
him in our conversations and in our imaginations, he must have been one of the
most extraordinary and inhuman freaks
that nature ever created. Instead of loving
life and believing in life, this artist we
talked about hated life and fled from it;
for that, indeed, was the basic theme of
many of the plays we wrote—[§] the
theme of the sensitive and extraordinary
person, the man of talent, the artist—crucified by life, misunderstood and scorned of
men, pilloried and driven out by the narrow bigotry and mean provincialism of the
town or village, betrayed and humiliated
by the cheapness of his wife, finally,
crushed, silenced, torn to pieces by the
organized power of *society* <the mob>.

Leaf 24

<¶> This artist that we talked about so
much, <on Eleventh street,> instead of
being in union with life, was in disunion
with it; instead of being near the world,
was constantly in a state of flight from it.

The world itself was like a beast of prey, and the artist like some stricken fawn <was> trying to escape from it. The total result of this was inevitable: it was to develope a kind of philosophy, an aesthetic, of escapism: it [*revised* escapism. It] tended to create in the person of the artist not only a special but a privileged character, who was not governed by the human laws that govern other men, who was not subject to the same desires, the same feelings, the same passions—who was, in short, a kind of beautiful disease in nature, like a pearl in an oyster. <¶> The effect upon such a person as myself may also be deduced: now [*revised* deduced. Now], for the first time, I was provided with a kind of protective armor, a kind of glittering and sophisticated defense which would shield my own self-doubt, my inner misgivings, my lack of confidence in my own powers, my ability to accomplish what I wanted to do. The result was to make me arrogantly truculent where my own desires and purposes were concerned. I began to talk the jargon as the others did; to prate about "the artist", and to refer scornfully and contemptuously to "the bourgeoisie"— the Babbitts and the Philistines—by which, I am afraid, we meant almost anyone who did not belong to the very small and precious province we had fashioned for ourselves. <¶> And, I am also afraid, that although we spoke [§] [*Seven diagonal pencil lines were drawn through the rest of this paragraph, presumably after Wolfe had made use of it in revised form.*] about "art", "the artist", and the work we wished

[*See YCGHA, p. 722.*]

Leaf 25

to do in phrases of devotion and humility; there was not so much of either one in us as there was of *snobbishness.* <the *scorn and* disdainful scorn of the small and precious snob.> We felt superior to other people, and we thought we were a rare breed; [*semicolon canceled, comma added*] <but we were not;> because one cannot be really superior without humility and tolerance and human understanding, and because one cannot be of a rare, [*comma canceled*] <and> higher breed without the talent and the power and the selfless immolation that true power and talent have, I [*revised* have. I] think most of us deceived ourselves—we [*revised* ourselves. We] were not the rare and gift [*hiatus*] people that we thought we were. <Stop>

Middle of Leaf 49 [See YCGHA, p. 723.]

<Start> All of my life *ever* since childhood, I had wanted what all men want in youth: to be famous <,> *and* to be loved. Now, I had had them both and—*there is not time or need here for apology or equivocation—I can only say that, so far as I was concerned,* <You had told me—here *the* our strange agreement of opposed polarity again—that I did not want them, that I only thought I did—I had found now that> they were not enough. And I think, if we speak truth, the same *has been* <is> true of every man who ever lived and grew, and had the spark of life and growth in him. It has never been dangerous to admit that fame was not enough—it has, indeed, by one of the greatest poet<s> who ever lived been called <the [*in Mrs. Campbell's hand*]> "last infirmity of noble minds"— but it has been, for reasons that I cannot

say, or *at any rate,* shall not mention here
—*been* dangerous to admit the infirmity of
love. *And yet—or so it seems to me, as a
simple product as* <*of [in Mrs. Campbell's
hand]*> *what I have myself known—there
may not have been a grown and a living
man who has never known the knowledge
that love brought to him; but there cannot
be a grown and a living man who has not
escaped the circle* <*precincts circle*> *of its
small tight whole.* <*precinct.*> [§] <¶>
Perhaps, *the* <love's> image *of it* may
suffice some people; perhaps, [*revised*
people. Perhaps,] as in a drop of shining
water, love may hold in microcosmos the
reflection of the sun and the stars and the
heavens and the whole universe of man;
and mighty [*revised* man. Mighty] poets
dead and gone have *declared* <said> that
this was true, and people have professed it
since—as [*revised* since. As] for myself, I
did not find it so, nor, plainly, do I think
a frog-pond, or <a> waldenpond [*revised*
Waldenpond] contains the image of the
ocean, even though there be water in both
of them. <¶> Both images, indeed, went
back through all the steps, the degrees, the
shadings, [*comma canceled*] of my education; and what we had been taught we
should believe. "Love is enough, though
the whole world be waning"—it may have
been, and yet I doubt it: as for myself, I
did not find it so.

And fame? <I had her too:> She [*revised* she] was another woman (of all love's
rivals <,> as I was to find, by a strange
paradox, the only one by women and by
love beloved)—and all her shifting images,
and all the guises of her loveliness, phan-

Leaf 50

[See *YCGHA,*
p. 726.]

tasmal, ghost-wise, like something flitting in a wood, I had dreamed of *her* since <my> early youth—until her image and the image of the loved one had a thousand times been merged together. Now, I had her, *and* <as [*in Mrs. Campbell's hand*]> she may be had—and it was not enough.

And yet, these [*revised* These] relics of the past were there. *The* <But life's> weather had soaked in, and yet, I was not conscious yet what seepings had begun, or where, in what directions, the channel of my life was *floating* <flowing>. I was exhausted from my labor, respiring from the race, conscious only as is an exhausted runner <that>, the race was over, the tape breasted, that <, in such measure,> he had won. This was the only thought within me at the time: the knowledge that I had met the ordeal a second time, and finally had conquered:—conquered my desperation and my own self-doubt, the [§] fear that I could never come again to a whole and final accomplishment.

[*See YCGHA, p. 727.*]
Leaf 51

The circle goes full swing. The cycle draws to its full close. For four months, emptied, hollow, worn out, my life marked time, while my exhausted spirit drew its breath. And then the world came in again, upon the floodtide of reviving energy—the [*revised* energy. The] world came in, the world kept coming in, and there was something in the world, and in my heart <,> I had not known *about* <of> before. <¶> I had gone back for rest, for recreation, for oblivion to that land which, of all the <foreign> lands that I *have* <had> known *beside my own,* I *have* loved best.

I had gone back to it in hours of desperate confinement, of brain-fagged searching, in retrospect, in imagination, and in longing a thousand times from the giant jungle web of Brooklyn. I had gone back to it a thousand times, as men in prison pent, haltered to all the dusty shackles of the hour, the confused traffics of clamorous days, the wearying grayness of inevitable Now, have longed for Cockaigne, <for> the haunted woods, the enchanted meadows, <and> the faery flood, the cloven rock. I had gone back to it in ten thousand dreams and memories of time and of desire —the sunken bell, the Gothic town, the plash of waters in the mid-night fountain, <the old Place,> the broken chime, and the blond flesh of secret, lavish women. I had gone back so in my memory and in desire a thousand times to Germany: and now that spring I was really there again— and no man ever had a happier or a more fortuitous *homecoming.* <return.>

Byron, they say, awoke one morning at the age of twenty-four, and found himself a famous man. Well, I had to wait some ten years longer, but the day came when I walked at morning through the Brandenburger gate [*revised* Gate] and into the enchanted avenues of the faery green Tiergarten, and found that fame—or so it seemed to me—had come to me. For two months or more I had been away from home, had seen *no* [§] no papers and had read no letters, had sought to find some easement, some slow and merciful release of the great coiled spring that was my mind and heart and very life that had been

Leaf 52

stretched to *the* breaking point for years;
and [*revised* years. And] I had found it
now in a series of oblivious wanderings
that had led from Paris to Kent and from
the *rumbling* <Romney> marshes up to
London, and from London to the flat
fecundity of Norfolk, and from Norfolk to
the small and tidy smugness of the Dutch,
and from Holland, as the train bore on,
across the great and fertile tillage of Westphalia, *and in* <to> Hannover <,> *that*
old time-haunted town, and there across
the kiefern-haunted forest of the North to
<vast> Berlin—and [*revised* Berlin. And]
now May had come again, and I walked
below the mighty blossoms of the great
horse chestnut trees, and through the Brandenburger gate [*revised* Gate], and
through the arcades of enchanted green,
and felt, like Tamerlane, that it was passing great to be a king, and ride in triumph
through Persepolis, [*comma canceled, dash
added*] and be a famous man.

After those long and weary years of
Brooklyn, *excavation,* and brute labor—of
desperation and the need for proof to give
some easement to my tormented soul—it
was the easement I had dreamed of, the
impossible faery, so impossibly desired,
and now brought magically to life. It was
—it seemed to be—the triumphant and the
glorious vindication of all that I had
thought my life could be, that man could
work for, or art achieve. The news of my
success at home had come to Germany—
where already I had been known for three
years, and had achieved celebrity—and
now, it seemed to me who had so often
gone a stranger and unknown to the great

cities of the world that now *that all* <*a the whole of it*> was mine—the <*revised mine. The*] <great> town, the whole world was my oyster. Letters were there for me, and invitations: it seemed they had been waiting for me—and for three weeks there was a round of pleasure, celebration <,> [§] the wonderful thrill of meeting in a foreign land and in a foreign tongue a hundred *old* friends, now for the first time known and captured—and May, and the cool nights, the glorious freshness of the air, the awakening of spring, the enchanted brevity of northern darkness, and glorious wine in slender bottles, and morning, and green fields, and pretty women—all of it was mine now, it seemed to have been created for me, to have waited for me, to exist and live in all its loveliness for my possession.

Three weeks passed so: *and* by [*revised so. By*] day there was the shining and the sapphire air, the horse chestnut trees, the singing sparkle of *exulted* <exultant> life that swept through me *and* across the town, so that at noon among the great crowds thronging the Kurfurstendamm, I also was a part of the green faery of the <great> Tiergarten park, and thence unto all crystal sparkles of Berlin, until I seemed to share it all, and all of it to be in me, as but a single, shining <and> exultant drop of water reflects and shares, and is a part of the million, million scallop shells of dancing light, and every lapping wave, and every white sail on the surface of *Awansay* <the Wawnsee>. <¶> And there would be the singing of the air by day, the un-

Leaf 53

[*See YCGHA, p. 728.*]

heard singing of the blood, and the great
crowds *on* <thronging> the Kurfurstendamm, the gay and crowded terraces of the
great cafes, and something, half-heard, half-
suspected, coming from afar, a few flung
seeds of golden *notes* <music> upon the
air, the sudden music of the tootling fifes,
and suddenly, the solid, liquid smack of
booted feet, and young brown faces shaded
under *their* steel *helmets* goose-stepping by
beneath the green arcades of the Kurfurstendamm, the army lorries rolling past
<,> each crowded with its regimented
rows of young, formal, helmeted, armfolded and ramrodded bodies, and laughter, laughter in the crowd, and laughter
rippling like a wave across the terraces of
Leaf 54   *the* great cafes <,> [§] and bubbling like
wine sparkles from the lips of all the pretty
women, [*comma canceled, dash added*] and
all the singing and the gold of it was mine.

But something happened—I was not prepared: too [*revised* prepared. Too] much
gray weather had soaked through into my
soul, <and I could not forget.> the [*revised* The] memory of unrecorded days,
the renaissance of brutal weathers, the excavation of the jungle trails; [*semicolon
canceled, dash added*] it all came back to
me again insensibly, soaked through the
shining brightness of that air, came
through the latches of those clacking
tongues, forced through at last its grim
imponderable into the contours of those
shining surfaces, the sense of buried meanings which not even May and magic and
the Kurfurstendamm could help. <¶>
Sometimes it came to me with *a* <the>

desperate pleading of an eye, and the
naked terror of a sudden look, the swift
concealment of a sudden fear: sometimes
[*revised* fear. Sometimes] it just came and
went as light comes, just soaked in, just
soaked in—words, speech and action, and
finally in the mid-watches of the night,
behind thick walls and bolted doors and
shuttered windows, the confession of un-
utterable despair, the corruption of man's   [*See YCGHA,*
living faith, the inferno of his buried an-   *p. 729.*]
guish—the spiritual disease and death and
strangulation of a noble and a mighty
people; [*semicolon canceled, period added*]
<¶> and [*revised* And] then day would   [*See YCGHA,*
come again, the cool glow of morning red,   *p. 730.*]
the bronze gold magic of the kiefern trees,
the still green pools of lucid water, the
faery stillness of the park and gardens of
the great Tiergarten street—but none of it
was the same as it had been before. For I
had become aware of something else in
life, as new as morning, and as old as Hell,
and now articulated for the first time in a
word, regimed now in a scheme of phrases
and a system of abominable works: and
[*revised* works. And] day by day the thing
soaked in, soaked in until everywhere, in
every life I met, and in every life I touched,
I met and saw and knew the ruin of its
unutterable pollutions; and it still came   *Leaf 55*
[§] in, it kept coming in, so known now
and understood at last beyond all depths
of intellectual understanding, since the
cancer and the root both came out of the
body I had *known and* loved.

And now, another layer had been peeled
off *of* the gauzes of the seeing eye; and
something had come into life that I had

never seen before, but that now once seen
and understood <,> I could never forget
or be blind to again. <Stop [*encircled*]>

APPENDIX II

THOMAS WOLFE LECTURES AND TAKES A HOLIDAY*

William Braswell

The first time I saw Thomas Wolfe I immediately accepted as fact all that I had thought of before as "the Wolfe legend." I had known that he was tall, but I had not expected to see a man six feet six inches tall who weighed over two hundred and fifty pounds. Nor had the pictures of him that I had seen shown the baldness at the back of his head or his tendency toward a large belly. But perhaps I was more surprised by his halting speech than by his appearance. He stammered a good deal, especially at the beginning of his address, with an impediment that reminded me more of Luke Gant than of Eugene. And his voice was so deep and throaty that the loudspeaker relayed it but poorly to the more distant of the three hundred people who had come to hear him. When he began to talk, I noticed some frowning and shaking of heads in the corner where I was, and one man sitting near by got up and moved closer to the speakers' table. I missed a word here and there, but never enough to lose the thread of thought. As Wolfe himself said by way of preface, he was not a good speaker. Yet he had a rugged force because of the naturalness, the sincerity, and the energy with which he spoke. As a matter of fact, his manner made perhaps as much impression as what he said.

The occasion at which he spoke was the Annual Literary Banquet at Purdue University on the evening of May 19, 1938. Just a handful in the audience knew that this was the

* © 1939 by *College English*. Reprinted from *College English*, October, 1939.

second such address that Wolfe had made. And of course no one suspected that this was to be the last public appearance of this huge, robust man who stood there straining at articulation and occasionally sawing the air with a heavy arm.

In response to the toastmaster's query about the place of writers in the world, Wolfe had begun by saying that the writer has just as definite a place to fill as the engineer, the lawyer, or the businessman. Writing, he affirmed, requires a man to work as hard as any other occupation. Humorously, he said that when he told his mother of having sold a story for fifteen hundred dollars, she replied: "Boy, you're the only one in the family who can make that much money without working." Just as his father's hands had developed calluses from working with mallet and chisel on stone, so his own fingers had become toughened by writing. Some people did not realize that a writer had to write and had to keep writing. Here Wolfe touched upon a matter that he later discussed at length in conversation: various groups had asked him to parade in front of this legation, to picket that concern, and the like, and he had refused, not because he was without sympathy and convictions in regard to the points at issue, but simply because he felt that, as a writer, he could spend his time better by writing. (In conversation he grew eloquent in ridiculing "old ladies" who continually invited him to costly tea parties where they voiced their pity in "ah's" and "oh's" and fished up a few dimes for Spanish orphans or for "the poor, poor Chinese.") He had never heeded the golden trumpets of Hollywood because he considered what he was doing more important than writing scenarios.

He emphasized the necessity of the writer's working with material that he knows thoroughly, and told how he himself had tried to write from his own experience. He admitted that he had made mistakes, one of which was that he had taken no pains to conceal the identity of certain people whom he had used as characters in his earlier works. When he had recently visited Asheville to see his mother, an old friend had taken him to task by saying: "It's all right to use a man as a character in a novel, but there's no need of giving the man's name, address, and telephone number!" His mistakes, he said, had taught him a great deal. As anyone familiar with the book may already have surmised, the essence of much that Wolfe said may be found in his *The Story of a Novel*.

One point that he made with some humor was that he could not tell anyone else how to write stories and articles that would make money because he did not know how to write them himself. He said that when he sold a story to the *Saturday Evening Post,* he thought his financial troubles were over: now that he knew what the *Post* wanted, all he would have to do to sell a story for a high price would be to sit down and turn one out according to his formula. But the next story he sent to the *Post* was rejected. This surprised him: he had thought this story would be "sure-fire," because it had the Civil War and everything else in it. He submitted it to several other magazines that paid unusually well; yet it was always returned. Finally it was accepted and published by the *Yale Review,* and he was very happy that it was, for he had great respect for that journal. Nevertheless, he added, he was not unaware that if the *Saturday Evening Post* had bought the story, he would have received about fourteen hundred dollars more for it.

Another anecdote that he told was about a hopeful Belgian woman who eagerly inquired when German soldiers invaded her town: "When do the atrocities begin?" The tight-lipped silence of a few elderly women was a futile rebuke amid the loud laughter that the story touched off. In fact, the audience was as responsive throughout the address as the speaker could have wished it to be.

At a brief reception held just after the banquet, Wolfe was pleased when complimented on his talk. Modestly repeating that he was no speaker, he went on to tell how a friend in New York had laughed at the idea of his being paid to give an address. His friend had exclaimed: "You know you can't deliver a speech!" Wolfe had replied: "No,

bit of profanity. He talked perhaps a little more than anyone else, but only because others led him to; he was quite
as good at listening as at talking, even asking, when he
missed a commonplace remark, "What?" or "What did
you say?" His ears were tuned to catch outside noises as
well as those in the room, for more than once he paused to
listen to the whistle of a train: "I've always liked to hear
them," he said. And as he conversed, his alert eyes, glancing
here and there, seemed to be taking in the whole room.
For several hours that night, and then the next afternoon,
when the circumstances were similar, he conversed on many
topics, most of them the trivial ones that academic groups
usually talk about.

One subject that he discussed with keen feeling was the
Spanish situation, which at the moment was causing much
international concern. He expressed strong sympathy for
the Loyalists and was perturbed by recent advances that
the Insurgents had made. His interest in politics in the
broad sense had increased greatly, he said, in the last year
or two. Affairs in Spain had moved him only a few days
before to write his first letter for publication to a periodical.
This letter, which appeared in the *Nation* for May 21,
referred to the report of General Franco's provisions to
care for the tourist trade in Spain during the coming summer and noted his ordering of "forty new and brightly
painted char-à-bancs" to convey the tourists:

> . . . In addition, it is understood that he has not only taken
> considerable pains in the work of restoring and preserving
> the most notable of the ancient ruins, but has also shown
> extraordinary ingenuity in the creation of new ones. For my
> part, although I by no means share the too general lack of
> veneration for the monuments of antiquity, I must confess
> that on the whole the evidences of the modern spirit are more
> exciting to me. If I had to choose between the two sets of
> ruins, I should be inclined to visit the new ones rather than
> the old.
>
> To mention but a few that have already suggested them-
> selves to my awakened curiosity—I should like to visit the
> various craters and ruined masonries throughout the town of
> Barcelona, paying particular attention to the subway entrance

where a bomb exploded and killed 126 men, women, and children. I should like to visit the ruins of Madrid, the ruined villages around Teruel; and being of a religious turn of mind, I should like to pay a visit of devotion to the chapel, a photograph of which was recently reproduced in the press, where General Franco's wife and daughter go to offer prayers for the success of the Defender of the Faith.

I have quoted this letter at length because it reveals so clearly the spirit that characterized Wolfe's many oral comments on the Insurgents.

He talked a good deal about contemporary authors. Not that he pretended to have read their recent publications, for he admitted that he had not read many books in the past few years. "I used to read everything," he said, "but now I don't read books; I'm too busy working on my own." His critical comments bore out this statement. He praised MacLeish's early work but did not know his later work. He called *A Farewell to Arms* a first-rate novel, but was not familiar with *To Have and Have Not.* He regretted that he had never had the opportunity to meet Ring Lardner, whom he praised for his canny insight into human nature and his fine satire on American types; he especially liked "The Golden Honeymoon." Having admitted the flaws usually pointed out in Dreiser, he expressed his admiration for the massive sincerity with which Dreiser had written about life. Of Masters' prose works he singled out the biography of Lindsay as an excellent book. He said that Lewis was one man who knew a great deal about American life and that Dos Passos was another. While he admitted Priestley's cleverness and skill, something in Priestley made him inveigh against British authors who, after a brief stay in America, say: "You know, old chap, what's wrong with you Americans is . . ." Of *The Ring and the Book,* which he had lately reread, he exclaimed with an emphatic swing of his arm, "God, what a book!" He told anecdotes about Masters, with whom he had had friendly talks in their hotel in New York, and related with especial relish Masters' curt, acid comments on certain celebrated but pompous authors. He chuckled as he gave an account of the curious fight between Hemingway and Eastman that took place in Scribner's editorial offices. It was in connection with this story that he spoke with such fondness of "Max" Perkins, who had aided him so in his craftsmanship and whom he was to make his literary executor.

One of the most amusing anecdotes that he told was about himself. When he was visiting James Thurber one evening shortly after the two had become acquainted, some member of the household was suddenly stricken with appendicitis and had to be rushed to the hospital for an emergency operation. During the operation and even afterward Wolfe stayed at the apartment, thinking, he said, that he was being "a great help," whereas he really was making Thurber more and more nervous. Finally, at a very late hour, when Wolfe was stretched out on a couch rosily enjoying still another drink, the mild-mannered Thurber left the living-room, only to return in a moment without coat and tie. With a look of melancholy and almost complete despair, he said to Wolfe: "I'm sorry, but I'll have to ask you to leave; I *must* get some sleep." Wolfe rose up and replied: "This is a h-h-h-hell of a way to treat a man. Is this what you call h-h-hospitality?" Someone more diplomatic than Thurber stepped in and gently persuaded Wolfe to leave. A week or two later a friend of Wolfe's told him of a cartoon that Thurber had drawn on the wall of a restaurant frequented by writers but as yet undiscovered by the public. Wolfe went to see the drawing. There on the wall was a large, hulking figure with Wolfe's features confronted by a little man standing on books piled in a chair, saying: "Mr. Wolfe, if you don't leave at once, I'm going to throw you out!"

If any of us had thought that Wolfe might prove difficult to associate with, as Eugene Gant sometimes was, his friendliness soon removed the fear. At the end of the second day he was calling all the group by their first names and insisting that they call him "Tom." There was no Rotarian hollowness in his doing this; his warm, natural manner would have made continued formality seem ridiculous. He appeared interested not only in those about him but also in people they mentioned. "Who is he?" "What does he do?" he would ask. Only once did I see him when he appeared oblivious of others, and that was when he stood for almost a minute looking into a mirror. He rubbed his hand over his face as a man does when he does not want to shave but thinks perhaps he ought to, he thrust forward his bottom lip in a characteristic way, and then he leaned over and looked deep into his eyes. What he was thinking, God knows.

Toward evening of the second day Wolfe began urging the whole group to go with him to Chicago, where he was to meet friends from the East. Everyone had been so kind to him, he said, that he wanted to give a big party: "I've just made three hundred dollars and y-y-you've got to help me spend it." He kept talking about that party.

Finally several of us set out in an automobile for Chicago, one hundred and twenty-five miles away. Speeding through the night with Wolfe, who was now in the gayest of moods, recalled the train ride so memorably described in *Of Time and the River*. "Look at this man drive!" he said; "look at this man drive!" He took part in all the group singing, whether he knew the words or not; and once he sang as a solo one of his father's favorites: "I Wonder Who's Kissing Her Now." But the song that delighted him most was the dwarfs' "Heigh-ho" song from *Snow White and the Seven Dwarfs*. This was to be his "theme song" for the week-end. He sang it even walking across a quiet street in Chicago, and, for his mediocre voice, with a ludicrously serious look on his face. And he kept singing it after some of its original charm had worn off.

Upon arriving in Chicago, we had a midnight supper, and then at Wolfe's request we drove to the Auditorium Hotel. "Ever since I traveled as a child with my mother," he said, "I've w-wanted to stay in this hotel, and now I'm going to do it." When we met him the next day to take him to lunch, he was exuberant about his large room overlooking Michigan Boulevard and the lake—"big enough for me to give my party in," he said. He was exuberant, too, because he had just seen his letter on Spain in the current issue of the *Nation*. When we were greeted at our friend's apartment, which we had visited the preceding night, Wolfe rumbled: "You can't keep the Wolfe from the door."

After lunch we listened intermittently to the broadcast of a baseball game between the New York Yankees and the Chicago White Sox. Wolfe had earlier grown so ecstatic about baseball—about its being the great American sport, the symbol of life itself—that someone who thought Wolfe must lately have written something about baseball had said teasingly: "That would sound good in a book, wouldn't it?" Wolfe had momentarily looked odd and smiled. Now he showed himself to be an ardent supporter of the Yankees. When someone mockingly reproached him for backing the strongest team in the big leagues, he defended himself by saying: "But the Yankees have always been my team—even b-b-back in the twenties when they had bad years." He admired their power, their sudden, spectacular feats. He was delighted by their one-to-nothing victory that afternoon and pretended to gloat over winning a twenty-five-cent bet on it.

During the course of the afternoon Wolfe wandered into the kitchen with his host and there shook hands with the colored servant, whom he talked with for several minutes about herself and her family. The effect of his friendliness upon her was not fully revealed until her mistress told her in the fall of Wolfe's death. Then she compared him with the world's heavyweight boxing champion, whom she knew personally: "What a pity!" she said with real emotion, "he was jus' like Joe Louis—so big, and yet so nice and kind."

When asked whether he wished to meet any of the local "celebrities," Wolfe replied: "This party's big enough for me." And two or three times when asked what he would like to do for entertainment, he answered: "G-g-gosh, I want to do whatever the rest want to do."

At his hotel room and later at a restaurant, Wolfe that evening got a great deal of pleasure from playing the attentive host. But at a dull cabaret which the party visited briefly he was particularly bored. It was here that he had one of those unpleasant experiences such as he recorded in "Gulliver," a sketch which tells how his height made him the butt of crude curiosity and jeers. When he went out to the bar to avoid having to watch the convulsive writhing of a woman dancer, a partially drunk man came up and tried to engage him in conversation. Although Wolfe at first looked very much annoyed, he covered up his irritation and patiently talked with the man for two or three minutes. But as Wolfe walked away, the man pointed after him with outstretched arm and, with a brazen, drunken grin, looked around at his neighbors, as if he wished all other normal, good fellows like himself to join him in laughing at this freak, this monstrosity. Fortunately, Wolfe was spared seeing this. And the only remark he made about the man's conversation was: "Oh, he didn't mean any harm. He was just drunk." It was also in this cabaret that Wolfe said in a hurt way to someone who paid the check: "You can't do this to me! Th-this is *my* party!"

Back at his room, just as the last of us were taking our leave, Wolfe did something so incongruous that it struck us as very amusing. After telling an inquiring maid at the door that he needed no more towels, he dashed to his bed, stepped up on it, took a couple of huge strides across it, and exclaimed: "My God! That was the ugliest face I've ever seen." Anyone who ever saw Wolfe can easily imagine what an astonishing sight he made as he walked upright across the bed.

The next afternoon Wolfe went with a small group to the Brookfield Zoo. As we drove through the West Side of Chicago, his eyes seemed to be recording all that lies behind the facade of Michigan Boulevard, which he called "the greatest shirt-front in the world." He craned his neck to see grotesque buildings, and he virtually counted the innumerable railway tracks. For all its ugliness, this sprawling, powerful city fascinated him as the metropolitan center of an abundant farming region. "The Middle West," he said, "reminds me of the back of a fat, sleek hog."

At the zoo he went from one exhibit to another with as much apparent delight as anyone else in the shuffling Sunday crowd. He was a bit disappointed because he could not find a baboon with so colorful a rump as one he had seen when he was a boy: "It was like a rainbow." And the baby giant panda was distressingly dull that day: all she did was to sit on a log and chew a stick. But the polar bears made up for any disappointment. Like almost everyone else who stopped before the open-air inclosure of these bears, Wolfe was fascinated by one that begged for favors from the crowd by climbing to a boulder above the pool, sitting back on his haunches, leaning slouchily with his "elbow" on an adjoining ledge, and then waving his right paw as he looked about at the people. Since the other bears were very adept at stealing the gifts, Wolfe laboriously threw several boxes of Cracker Jack before he felt that he had sufficiently rewarded this genial performer.

Watching and listening to the people also pleased Wolfe. He smiled at some of their actions and their remarks, such as one man's saying to another about the giraffes: "Oh, but you know they're highly exaggerated." The remark of a colored woman to her companions, "Heah some mo' bea's ovah heah," caused him to smile and say: "Isn't this a great country!" On being told that it was up to him to express that greatness, he said: "I'm going to do all I can, but the rest of you will have to help." Thus colloquially he affirmed what he had said in closing *The Story of a Novel*:

> . . . Out of the billion forms of America, out of the savage violence and the dense complexity of all its swarming life; from the unique and single substance of this land and life of ours, must we draw the power and energy of our own life, the articulation of our speech, the substance of our art.

At dinner that evening, at the famous old German restaurant the Red Star Inn, Wolfe told how during his long visits in Germany he had come to love that country—not the government, which he denounced, but the people, for their cleanness and their solid ways of living, and the land, for its beautiful forests and valleys. And at the end of the meal he insisted: "Now everybody *m-must* have German pancake for dessert."

When we finally said goodbye to Wolfe, he spoke again of his intention to go to the Northwest after visiting in Colorado, and then to stop in Chicago for another party on his way back East. Standing there in front of his hotel, he was the only one in the group who did not seem a little tired; his energy and exuberance gave one no thought of anything but life. We later heard that just before leaving Chicago on the "Zephyr" he was full of boyish anticipation in regard to his first ride on a streamlined train; he even reserved a berth, knowing how little comfort it would give him. "By God, I m-m-might as well go the whole hog," he said.

From Denver he wrote on May 31 to his host in Lafayette:

> I'm late in writing you to say hello and thanks again; and to let you all know that I think about you and the good time we had together, and the hope that we will do it again. I've been here almost a week—I came for just a *day!*—the whole town has been swell to me—so swell that for the first few days we just eliminated sleep as a despicable luxury. But I'm beginning to feel ironed out again, and if I can only keep my fingers off the cursed quill for another week or two—which I doubt!— I should be in fairly good shape for the struggle when I go back East. Am still resolute in my intention to push on to the Northwest, although my friends here now lift their eyebrows and smile skeptically when I speak of it! And I'm still hoping to stop over in Chicago long enough to see you all again. Meanwhile, I send love and best wishes to you all.
>
> Sincerely,
Tom Wolfe
>
> P.S. Take care of the polar bears!

The next news was that Wolfe was critically ill with pneumonia in Seattle. After this came a report of his journey across the continent to Johns Hopkins in the care of his mother and sister. And then his death.

INDEX

This book was set in Linotype Baskerville, a face known as a traditional design bridging the gap between "old-style" and "modern-style" faces. The book was printed by C. E. Pauley and Co., Indianapolis, on 60 lb. Glatex Antique Offset stock and bound by Heckman Bindery, North Manchester, Ind. Frontispiece engraving by Rheitone, Inc., Indianapolis. The jacket was designed by Moroni St. John and printed by offset lithography by Krieger, Ragsdale and Co., Evansville, Ind.